ANCHOR BOOKS

As We Look Upon This World

Edited by

Laura Rogers

First published in Great Britain in 2005 by
ANCHOR BOOKS
Remus House,
Coltsfoot Drive,
Peterborough, PE2 9JX
Telephone (01733) 898102

SB ISBN 1 84418 398 X

Foreword

Anchor Books is a small press, established in 1992, with the aim of promoting readable poetry to as wide an audience as possible.

We hope to establish an outlet for writers of poetry who may have struggled to see their work in print.

The poems presented here have been selected from many entries, and as always editing proved to be a difficult task.

I trust this selection will delight and please the authors and all those who enjoy reading poetry.

Laura Rogers
Editor

Contents

NATURE'S JEWELS

It is early morning
There's an early morning mist
A dew that came down overnight
The earth has gently kissed
In the hedgerows, spiders' webs
Like pearl necklaces are seen
The dew-like droplets, hang in rows
In this nature's jeweller's scene
The sun is trying to break through
To melt this misty scene
This vale of whiteness everywhere
Is as if, in some sort of dream
I notice as I am walking
This dew now hangs on me
A vapour now clings to my clothes
I can clearly see
Nature's sprinkler, dampens everywhere
To clean and feed the plants
A gentle breeze is getting up
The droplets now perform a water dance
They then break free, and run as one
And fall upon the ground
Those jewel-like droplets that once were seen
Are nowhere to be found.

B Page

SUNRISE/SUNSET

Deep Crimson sun with golden hue
Will rise just as it sets - give new
Dimension to a tinted sky
Which tips with pink the landscape's sigh

As focused rays on dawn's grey light
Or evening's close, come into sight
To penetrate through leaf and bough,
On woven thatch and furrowed plough

Give credence to a force on high
Which human kind will testify
Is nature's enigmatic way
Of structuring each life-long day

Jo Lewis

FEBRUARY SKEIN

They come in the pre-dawn mist
A murmuring to turn the ear, haunting, eerie
And then an emblem outline in the sky

A leader orchestrates, then leaderless
They drift like flotsam
Ever onwards, eastwards to
Their summer home, for
Rich pastures of renewal
Beckon on endless time

A cacophony of sound
Calls stragglers to the
Arrowhead snaking restless
Ever unifying a spirit born on generations passing

And then the murmuring reincarnates waning, waning
New leaders leading into the rising sun

M C Davies

THE STORM

A gale-force wind is blowing,
Torrential rain falls fast,
Hailstones ping against
The windowpanes,
And cover the grass.
Skies black as ink,
Thunder rolls across the sky,
Lightning flashes,
High gusts of cold air blow
Slates off the rooftops.
Trees sway rapidly back and fore,
Their branches broken.
Birds cry as they desperately try
To fly forward and get nowhere.
Fences lifted, blown like paper.
Waves wash over the promenade,
White horses ride them
Throwing wide their spray.
Steams and rivers overflow,
Fields deep in water, mud everywhere,
The grass blown into a sea of waves.

Doreen Petherick Cox

THE DEEP DREAM SONG

(The song of the birds)

Sung by the ancient birds
The sound verse
Created the universe.

Songs within songs
Life within life
Ring, rhythm and rhyme
Through layers of time

The deep dream song
Is yours and mine.
Everyone, everything
Forever and always
For better, for worse
Let us all sing
The sacred verse.

I lift my guitar
And strum
The deep dream song
For everyone.

Graham Peter Metson

THE SHORTEST MONTH

Deep-cleansed by the piercing frost;
Gently bleached by snow;
Fully refreshed by life-giving rains,
The earth is awaiting - expectant - on tiptoe -
The wondrous upsurge of spring.

Already the catkins of alder and hazel
Tremble, like tassels caressed by a breeze;
While water-rich ditches awaken the celandine -
Urge the wild arum to unfurl its leaves.
Nearby, in the churchyard, a sheltering tombstone
Has prompted a primrose to smile once again;
While late Christmas roses and aconites golden,
With drifting white snowdrops, are braving the wind.

A bright, sunny day sets the birds all a-flutter -
Eager to mate and start building a nest;
While small woodland creatures, tucked deep 'neath the hedgerow,
Stir in their winter sleep, sensing each change.
For the shortest of months brings confusion of weather -
Chill of the arctic - warmth of the sun;
The sharpness of frost - the whisper of snowflakes;
A gale - or a storm - or a flood.

But *with* what it brings comes a foretaste of spring,
So - although we may soon wish it gone!
February - the *clean* month -
The redeemed earth month -
Is a month to be welcomed - and loved.

V J Havis

NATURE'S MEDICINE

If ever life gets you down,
Walk in a wood and look around.
There's natural medicine to be found,
Follow a river's winding way,
Carpets of bluebell, and fields of hay,
Turn blackness into a sunny day.
Leaves and flowers of assorted hue,
Walk on earth damp with dew,
Aromas of bittersweet fungi musk
Blending with acorn and beechnut husk.
'Nature's medicine' all of these,
Squirrels run up into the trees
That sway gently in the breeze.

Hear the trill of a songbird,
The sweetest sound ever heard.
This 'prescription', a walk in the wood,
Is guaranteed to make you feel good.
Not tried it yet? Well you should!
If you try it you will see
Better 'medicine' could not be,
'Medicine' that works, natural and free,
It's the one that works for me!

Sheila Walters

WINTER'S SUNDAY

Sunday quiet descends upon the town,
A damp mist is swirling, like cloud across the ground.
White frost is glistening on the slate roof tops,
Where silent as a ghost, the white cat stops.

The dog runs down the garden, with a growl,
The cat makes hasty exit, with much spitting and a scowl.
Then all the birds come swooping to the earth,
Pecking for the worms beneath the turf.

A thrush sits on the wall now, beside a shivering sparrow,
Then darts down past the holly tree, swifter than an arrow.
Small blue tits peck at nuts hung from thin branches,
While doggy's there, the cat will take no chances.

After lunch we stroll down to the park,
In winter early, for it soon grows dark.
The ducks' webbed feet skid on the frozen lake
As they peck at crumbled bread and broken cake.

Then the gulls come screaming through the frosty air,
And swoop down in their hordes to take their share.
The dog stands watching them, with wondering eyes
And listens to their shrill and plaintive cries.

Yet soon the fleeting daylight will be gone,
So home we go, to put the kettle on,
Then doggy flops before the fire's glow,
While the cat slinks to the roof and crouches low.

Frankie Shepherd

An Uneasy Day

The howling wind attacked the cringing earth,
Trees bent, crackling branches fell on sodden ground,
A hardy sheep sheltered by the dry stone wall,
The cawing crows' startled calls were drowned.

Muddied waters rose above the river's banks,
Lakes newly-formed spread across the grass,
Rotting leaves had blocked the roadside drains,
Floods swirled, cars could no longer pass.

Nervous people scurried to their homes,
Market traders filled their vans with stock,
Frightened children, noses pressed to windowpanes,
Watched nature's fury as she ran amok.

Gradually sun rays broke through weary clouds,
Strong winds abated, rain began to cease,
Blue skies again, birds merrily chirped,
Stoically, the sheep shook its bedraggled fleece.

Elaine Beresford

Tsunami Assault

A twisted face looked out at me filled with such horrendous grief
Such shocking pain and heartache that truly beggars belief.
'Midst the chaos I saw kindness as mankind reached out to give a hand.
Tears and help intermingled as aid marched across the land.
So many children now are gone and many a mother weeps.
The young, the old, all were swept away, tsunami drew
so many in its sweep.
With strong support those hearts will heal, the river of tears will cease.
Hope lies in the future where they shall have flowers
instead of a wreath.
Only time shall make it clearer, time alone will ease the pain.
Sweet memories shall cover the sadness and life shall be
worth living again.
Meanwhile all must do their grieving, no need to hold back a tear.
Let the tears flow in their season for the lost who are no longer here.
I have one thing I cannot do, I cannot cry out, 'Why?'
How could I ever understand why I've seen so many innocents die?

Rosie Hues

COLOUR TIME

Autumn gold is in the leaves,
Reflecting the sun it receives
On those glorious days
When the skies are clear,
And rain has gone other ways;
Colours are bright and very near,
Orange and red also in the trees,
Seen with the last of the bees;
Berries too reflect their worth,
On which birds feed to stimulate birth;
Dahlias and others still bloom,
Only to die back very soon.

There's a nip in the air,
To make you think very clear,
That winter is round the corner, near,
But all is not down the sink,
For winter heathers and others go
Displaying yet a different show;
Each season brings its own rewards,
Suiting weather conditions that it accords;
Even snow enhances the scene,
Though to some it's cold and mean,
That can be countered too,
With woollies and a fur-lined shoe.

The weather we cannot create,
How we deal with it is ours to dictate,
So make the most of every clime,
Select the best that suits you fine
And enjoy it.

George Beckford

THE RIVER

Oh! Mighty river how flow you on,
Gliding gently whilst all is union,
Thro' thick, lush meadows of pure delight,
Into the deep, dark, unknown night,
Where leafy rustled, breeze-filled woods,
And stars twinkle as elegant stood
Sweet angels playing amongst the clouds,
Fleeting softly with wings full-bowed,
Towards the cities of Gothic splendours,
They face changeth from green promontory land,
To smoky chimneys and capital bland,
To leave behind your wistful memories,
Oh! Mighty river how flow you on.

Mel Price

SABRINA GODDESS OF THE SEVERN

Gulls, pink flushed with summer's dawn sun
Tranquil Severn, shallow, still.
Waiting for the tide with its rushing run
Swamping spacious sands and struggling to the fill.

Now fully gorged and satisfied.

Sabrina holds her breath and sighs
Turns and lazily floats another way
Gliding gulls voice their calling cries
Watching
As she caresses the curving bay.

Flora Denning

SEASONS

The flowers and trees are to shed their leaves
What beauty, what wonder of nature
To settle down after the autumn breeze
To be content in winter's pleasure

Then to spring we look forward again
With hope in our hearts for the unexpected
Through summer we anticipate
Until once again autumn makes us feel dejected

Did we not fulfil our dreams
Whilst the sun shone brightly?
Do we once again have to face winter and cope
Be content until spring returns our hope?

If this is life then I must be
Resigned to live life ever free
But I know when spring comes once again
My tears will vanish in the rain

Thoughts of the past will slip from my mind
As once again my hopes begin to climb
As the trees are full of blossom and leaves
So I wish my life to be content with only these.

Kathryn E Needham

SEASCAPE

You've never seen peace,
till you've seen a calm sea,
with a mist, eternally drifting.

With never a wave,
an endless grey grave,
a haze, that's always just lifting.

But the fury and torment,
of a sea once so dormant,
in the midst of a living gale.

That throws up walls,
of water, that falls,
on those intrepids, that sail.

The wind that screeches,
as waves thrash the beaches,
in the frenzy of wrath to break free.

Such illimitable power,
makes brave men cower
and mankind, gasp in wonder to see.

Harry Lyons

An Ode To Nature

Nature is the life-force of every living thing,
Superior man,
The tiny ant,
Was wrought by nature's mighty plan.
Too many to mention,
That's not my intention,
The beauty is sublime,
When hurricanes blow
When deep in snow
Nature is profound
Some thank God for nature's gifts
In every season of the year,
Just look around and you will find
Eternal Earth is nature's child.

M Andrews

INTO THE GARDEN

Why did he leave me, my errant lover?
Does he not care, now my life has no meaning?
Don't beckon me, pond, I have no more interest,
You must struggle with spring; I have no will to help
But I see movement stirring your water,
The toads have returned, laying strings of black pearls.
Entwined around fronds of tender green plantlets
Such urgency there, no time to reflect.
What compelled me to step into the garden
And witness the birth of this year's new spring?
Taking strength from the toads' instinct for living
Dispersing the mists of self-pity.

Jill Mackness

In The Hedgerows Of Surrey

Bright the flowers that twist and ramble
O'er the thicket, hedge and bramble,
There the honeysuckle sweet,
With the bindweed, will compete.
Both bloom, enhancing Heaven's light,
One orange, t'other purist white.
Both grow at will, out of control,
Neither is fit for vase or bowl,
Both climb, entwine another's stem,
Yet one we love and one condemn.

Robert Bowhill

ELEGANCE PERFECTED

In pools of shimmering waters, a gentle ripple forms,
It swirls around the edges, and laps along the shore.
A movement on the surface that barely makes a stir,
Reveals an elegant creature as just a glimpse of fur.

It dives and sinks in the water, like a falling stone,
Secures its catch of fish or eel, and devours it alone.
In swathes of mist he disappears, and falls beneath the waves,
Into the depths of darkness, exploring hidden caves.

The morning sun shines at last, and sweeps away the clouds.
Flowers open majestically, that nature has endowed.
The otter leaves the water to places of retreat,
And waits for the moonlight, for his next nocturnal feast.

Catherine Lambert

AND THE STONE CRIES OUT

You were once part of a bigger soul
Then circumstances set you free
You are now responsible for your own soul
Layers of self are rhythmically washed away
To lie as part of the infinite dust
You're disappearing
You cry out
An exile
You are then placed on the high tide line
Sun bleaches you
Wind moulds you
Rain washes you
Feet kick you
Hands caress you
You are taken to another's sanctuary
You are disappearing
You cry out
An unforgetful exile
You are not responsible for your own soul
Here there are dark shadows of soul
It has all been pre-destined
The pureness of truth caresses the soul
You cry out
You will become infinite
A long journey of crying.

Hilary Jean Clark

WANDER

O fishes would you welcome me,
If I fell into your deep, deep sea?
And if swim my arms could do not well,
Would you me where to rest at night, so tell?
And eagles as they soar so high,
My friends be, if but I could fly?
Then if my legs be not too strong,
To carry me more miles along,
Would the grass that grows e'er 'neath my feet,
Provide me with a noon-day seat?
Would that mountain up in the sky,
Let me it climb, and with my eyes to try
To see whate'er had been unseen,
And look back at where I had been?
Through the sun and rain and clouds that run their race,
It isn't such a bad old place!

Alistair McLean

REDWOOD ON A MOUNTAINTOP

I smell the redwood
as its essence
escapes the forest,
then lands on my nose.

Its smell is the
humus of life.
It speaks of years
gone by
and days to follow.

It promises
everlasting life
as it stands with peers
on a mountaintop.

Conifers soak up the rainwater
and absorb the sunlight
in their fruitless race
to be so grand.

Elizabeth C Millar

THE NATURE WALK

The children went walking right into the wood
Stepping shiny new wellies deep into the mud.
Their teacher, Miss Hughes, had set them a task
To seek signs of the autumn in each thing they passed.
First up were the trees, leaves of red, yellow and gold,
Their boughs standing out so black and so bold.
Then came the toadstools so colourful and bright
Tommy jumped on a puffball - gave himself such a fright!
Blackberries, hazelnuts - here there were feasts
For squirrels and blackbirds and other fine beasts.
They all ran for conkers so shiny and brown
Each hoping to win the conker champ's crown.
With smoke in the air and clouds filled with rain
It had soon become time to walk back again.
With faces aglow, and eyes very bright
They all marched away filled with nature's delights.

Jayne Shepherd

TSUNAMI

Did the Earth move for you?
Titanic tectonic tensions
An ocean torn asunder.

Did the Earth move for you?
Rolling, writhing, reaching
Such might, but yet no thunder.

Did the Earth move for you?
Crashing, smashing, lashing
And poor souls pulled down under.

Did the Earth move for you?
Heaving, speeding, seething
An ocean's massive murder.

Did the Earth move for you?
Giving, grieving, needing
To mend the heart and hunger.

Did the Earth move for you?
Oceans of emotion
Respond to this cruel wonder.

Did the Earth move for you?
Let us all confess
We gave our pennies and our pounds
In cities, villages and towns
I think this time we did it right,
I think this time the answer's yes
All of you, yes, even me
We'll remember all our days
The day of the tsunami waves.

Martin Harris Parry

TSUNAMI

Waves, life crushing, careless in their tumultuous sweep
Of dire destruction, unpitying in the surge of
Primal power, have trashed the monuments of
Human self-regard.
The raw supremacy of natural force makes
No exceptions nor forgives.

Tsunami, sweet sounding word, belies the havoc
That it hurls upon the ocean's verge, where thousands
Perish at its cruel whim and men's solidities
Are nullified by water's mastery.

The sea was kind to fisherfolk and those who plied
Their trades along the coasts. Visitors cavorting
On its surface or below or idling on
The shore were happy guests and unaware . . .
So many lost and why?

There is no answer and in that vacuum lies
Our pride, which calls for reasons and a moral cause
For each effect. The grinding of tectonic plates
Beneath the sea, the following catastrophe,
Corpse-littered streets, the salt drenched ruins of uncounted
Towns and places where the innocent had lived and
Died, all tell us nothing. It simply happened.

So let us grieve but ask no further questions
And in that silence learn humility.

Rex Baker

AUTUMN

A fairy's lacy curtain, hung with a million minuscule gems,
A spider's web in the morning mist, in the bushes strung from
the stems,
A glitter trail, left by a wandering snail,
In the quiet hours before it's light,
And as the sun rises, what more surprises will I find for my
eyes' delight?
A bright bloom that yesterday was only a bud,
Just beginning to split,
Now a crimson rose shows off its petals before the next storm's
due to hit,
And after the downpour and the wind's fierce roar,
And lightning splitting the sky,
The quiet returns and the spider learns the art of spinning anew,
Amidst a scattering of petals beneath a rosebush,
Where a brilliant bloom once grew!

Christine May Turner

Snow

Weary of worldly intrusion,
I welcome the coming of snow,
slowly and softly subduing
the disturbance of alien sounds.
A landscape bereft of motion
but for the brisk blackbird
and rooks in the upper distance,
wheeling and whirling as cinders,
from a windswept bonfire blown.
Still, stand the mute-black woodlands
deep in their winter sleep,
and the white-polled hedgerows bestowing
calm and brooding enclosures
for the shrouded roads between.
But this beauty is an illusion,
for the coming thaw will bring
the movement of men and machinery
at work on the new bypass.

Tony King

The Wave Of Destruction

With one almighty roar
They were snatched from the treelined shore
We evolve from the sea
Now it's reclaimed loved ones from you and me.
People that we never knew
Have touched our hearts.
What can we do?
Women, children, men from all nations.
No discrimination.
Is there a God who can cause such pain?
This question will be asked time and again.
Maybe He needs them more than we know
From this natural disaster maybe a better understanding will grow.

Their lives have not been in vain
A legacy of love will remain
It has brought nations together
This strange power of Mother Nature.

Christine Hardemon

TSUNAMI TERROR

I look at such terror and try hard to believe,
That nature's raw wrath is beyond us to conceive.
So many faces snatched, dragged away,
Parents in Hell, kiddies snared, stolen from arms of love,
On Hell's Earthly day.
Confused feelings, is God really there?
To allow such anguish and pain,
Haunted stares.
We go to our churches, whatever they be,
And give money to help those surviving the sea.
Such terror on faces that stare back, broken forever,
So many wars created by man unable to live together.
If that wasn't enough raw nature plays with our minds,
Such harrowing stories from souls born of mankind.
Every life stolen away to Earth's swirling seas,
Does God see these images that Earth's sea does unleash?
We watch and we cry, families, generations, deceased.
Parents contorted with pain, of kiddies now gone to the sea, claimed.
So many souls float back, battered and maimed.
If life comes to test us and leaves us such pain,
The souls of so many tortured and dead, images remain. Always.

Kath Watkiss

A Winter's Ride

Horses' hoof prints,
like hollow echoes,
iron shod
on iron ground,
canter through the
frozen landscape,
fractured by the
bubbling ice.

Past bare fields fixed
in painful sunlight,
through meadows furred
in needling ice;
every grass blade
forged in sharp frost,
glazed in winter's
rigid stare.

As streaming sunshine
strengthens through the
cut-glass coldness,
hoof prints deepen;
smudging out to
blurring edges
as heavy earth begins
to steam.

Sarah Nichols

SPRING

The sun shines brightly,
The rain falls slightly.

The nights are getting lighter,
The weather is getting brighter.

Buttercups create a carpet of yellow,
Making meadows look pleasant and mellow.

Everywhere is nice and colourful,
The weather is no longer doleful.

Easter is on its way,
Chocolate eggs will be eaten all day.

Spring is here at last,
Winter has finally passed.

Summer will be after this,
This will be a spring that I am going to miss.

Gordon Collinson

FANTASY

In Lothlorien the bark of the tree turns silver.
After the long winter when the leaves have not fallen
But turned to gold,
The spring comes and the new green opens,
The boughs are laden with yellow flowers
And the floor of the wood is golden.
There is a feeling of restlessness, excitement
And desire for adventure and novelty.
A season of new growth between the winters
And the summer,
Beneath the eaves of the wood
Our hearts were glad it was springtime.

Beverly Maiden

WINTER HAS COME

I can see through the branches of the trees
The anger of the clouds against the sky;
The leaves have all but dropped to earth,
In fact as I look I see the last leaf fly.
As you and I walk across the common
Our feet beat down on hard grey turf
Frosted from the night before,
Which gives an armour to the surface of the earth
To save her fruitful depths from growing raw.
And returning to the village
We find the chimneys smoking
And curtains drawn.
Winter will shut us in.
You beckon me to share the glow of open hearth
Where burning logs throw shadows on the wall.
You smile - although you watch me make myself at home,
We know that in our hearts will lie an uneasy pain
Till spring heralds summer and leaves are on the trees again.

Paul Gardner

WINTER

Autumn soon to winter turns
And some fires still in homestead burns.
Though central heating be the norm
To keep us warm from wind and storm.
On cold days when men venture forth
Stout boots, thick hose and overcoat
And scarves to shield against the storm,
Thick gloves to keep our fingers warm
And woolly hat protects our head,
We all appreciate the bed.
And there we through the night, abide
While snow falls down and frost outside.

White, smooth, attractive looks the snow
Through the window while cold winds blow,
Till that which looked so smooth and lush
Trod down by man becometh slush.
Slippery slush and ice below
Makes our feet and fingers glow.
Frostbite and chilblains doth appear
And accidents occur down here
By road and rail, by land and sea
And cause sadness to you and me.

And yet young children like to play,
To build a snowman every day,
Throw snowballs at one another
To Mother, Father, Sister, Brother - and hope
To run toboggan down a slope.
But there's a serious side to snow,
Good properties for Earth below.
God in his wisdom sent it down
To feed the Earth and glory crown.
To bring forth in the coming year
A rich harvest in hope and fear.

P Mathias

WINTER ONCE MORE

As I walk outside, the cold grips my naked hands,
The wind stings my puffed cheeks,
The leaves and twigs crackle under my feet,
It's winter once more.

From the brick-built chimneys billows smoke,
Pheasants scurry across the country lanes.
Birds migrate in hoards through the dull sky,
It's winter once more.

On my return, the smell of stew meets my cold nose,
The fire's roaring to warm my bitter hands,
A nice mug of cocoa thaws me out,
It's winter once more.

Carol Paxton

FESTIVE LIGHT

Suddenly a match's flame makes skipping sparks
spurt into subtle flaming jets,
then fizzle to flash more boldly
into a wild, orange-skirted dance.

Dried brown and brittle leaves
lie scattered among logs in a wide barred fire;
dove-grey smoke, cloudy as a valley's mist,
drifts among snapping hearth bound twigs.

Dabs of brilliant lemon leap to spaces
above the waxing warmness of the sticks,
which flame quickly in spurting bursts
to release the secrets of a living fire.

The leaves curl and vanish into vivid scarlet
like flaunted scarves waved by frantic fans;
then glowing splinters of burning wood
tock and tick as though old winter's clock.

Then is that moment when the wax is scented
as a taper's flame nears a festal candle,
raised wicks now bow to the flickering light
before it's snuffed above the fruity spices.

The indoor light enlivens with amber whirls
pushing wisps of flint smoke spiralling high;
a door closes, the guests are seated
as candlelight quick silvers the cutlery.

The largest candle commands the grandest holder
and stands above the others like their lord;
the diners fill the shadows with their laughter
settling around the festive crackling logs.

Dennis Marshall

Harsh Winter

A robin swoops down onto a stump covered in ivy
frost forms making a picture card scene.
The robin fluffs out his feathers and flies to some fat balls
hanging on a veranda that might keep him alive this winter.
A fox skulks across the field, head cast down, he spots
a landing crow and hastens his pace only to get mobbed.
A large rabbit appears from the hedgerow and sits up to look
around, whilst another eagerly eats the spoils of leftover winter cereal.
A buzzard flies over and swoops down upon the rabbits, who leap to
cover in the hedge, the bird rises and glides away like a kite in the wind.
As I sit quietly, only inches away, a young deer pops out its head
from the trees, followed by another, they are young hind,
a gust of wind sends their legs kicking, as they run back into the safety
of the forest glade.
A tree opposite, covered in red berries, is ambushed by birds,
a blackbird sings a beautiful song, then flies along the hedgerow as
though looking for a nesting place for her young in the spring.

Jean Bailey

SPRING'S REUNION

Spring has taken winter's place,
spring has welcomed us with her bright, warm, smiling face,
everyone is delighted,
God's creatures are all reunited,
bluetit, chaffinch, thrush and starling
sing their sweet song to welcome spring,
in the blue skies, flies a cuckoo,
wild forget-me-not, violet,
buttercup, sweet lavender blue,
crocuses, tulip, narcissus, daffodil
grow in spring,
a butterfly, such a graceful, gentle thing,
a ladybird crawls on colourful flowers, in gardens she dwells
enjoying the warm, sunny spells,
a bumblebee collects sweet nectar from flowers,
white, pink, blue, orange and red,
a spider spins his web,
for the long warm, sunny days ahead,
squirrels scamper and chase,
lambs frolic in the countryside's wide open space,
bunnies black, brown and white
in spring's delight,
hatching chicks,
as the spring clock ticks,
a hedgehog uncurls, he comes out of winter's hibernation
in spring's celebration,
now they're all one big happy family
in spring's harmony.

Joanna Marie John

A Long Winter

Whistling wind,
Sharp as a sword.
Snowstorms gather
In no time at all,
Howling a sign of danger,
Shivering trees shed their
Gold icicles across
Like fighting Vikings.

Alan Hattersley

Winter Visitor

Black, black, bird.
Perfectly black, perfectly quiet.
Sits in silver.
Through his golden circle pours the world.
And I am fixed and poured.
Or, does he rather see the pane
As old friends see the years?
Reflections, distorted.
Beautiful blackbird,
Perfectly black, perfectly quiet,
Caged in silver.
You sit in peace and curiosity,
Forgetful of your message.
You're not to blame.
This season has been cold and long.
Silence left alone grows strong,
Numbs the mind and takes away the song.

Lydia Dier

THE END FOR ME!

I'm no linguist, but it's as plain as plain, to me
The ninth day, or the eleventh hour, means November, you'll see.
Well, an octogenarian has lived eighty years, the eighth month
of the year
shouldn't be August but October; December, September, ten
and seven, or am I queer?

Someone once said, some hundreds of years back in history,
the year used to end in the coldest month, usually February.
To begin once again, stride forth toward spring, it seems
appropriate, somehow, March
is the start, not the middle of winter, to signify the New Year,
when the worst has passed.
Whether this causes ire, from those satisfied with their counting of days,
towards me for disturbing them, I cannot explain it, I have no
calculating ways
but the sound of light rain I just love to hear.

For me it would have to be the first day in January, my eleventh hour,
the last opportunity for me, before I begin to flower.
Isn't it said; those who are dead are 'pushing up daisies?'
But there isn't any land about me to grow anything, it's as bleak
as bleak can be.
Given half a chance I'd allow them to grow, for there's nothing so
pretty as daisies, for me.

Gerasim

CASTELL COCH

Castell Coch is a castle in Wales
In a place with a strange sounding name,
Yet the grandeur of that magical spot
Only attests to its fame.

Not old in the sense of 'ancient'
I suppose just a folly in part,
But you would have to be made of stone
Not to take it to your heart.

The Red Castle of Tongwynlais
Sits on the side of a hill,
The backdrop for many a filmset
The memories linger there still.

This wonderful fairytale castle
Impressive both inside and out,
Simply tugs at the heartstrings
Of that, there is really no doubt.

Once seen it is never forgotten
Like a fantasy sublime,
Castell Coch's proud reputation
Is fondly wrapped in time.

Moira Wiggins

CLEOBURY MORTIMER

Cleobury town with its crooked steeple
Cleobury town with its friendly people:
This is where I went to school
I was no scholar but I was no fool.

Those were good times, so I'm told,
When Titterstone blew and I was cold:
Snow drifting over tops of hedges
Lads tumbling headlong off their sledges.

Cleobury lanes in spring were blessed
With scented violets, and butter-yellow primroses dressed,
Hedgerow banks with clumps of colour
Amongst white daisies in a patchwork cover.

Come and visit Cleobury town,
Spare an hour - walk up and down,
Say 'hello' to the friendly people
Who live around the crooked steeple.

N M Beddoes

Picture Perfect

Wish you were here,
Here you would wish
You could stay forever.

Picture perfect,
A perfect picture.
Rolling hills,
Beautiful beaches,
Breathtaking cliffs,
Rugged rock pools,
Waves wistfully, softly
Caressing the sand.

People laughing,
Relaxed, carefree,
Children playing,
No shackles,
No worries,
Just being
And enjoying.

Picture perfect
A perfect picture,
A snapshot in time
Before back to reality.

Wish you were here.

Here you would
Wish you could
Stay
Forever.

Catherine Pasek

Holiday Time

It's holiday time
So here we are
On a boat trip with music, chatter and fun,
Do come and join us
Where smugglers once ran.

Off the side of the boat
People dive in,
Laughter and cheer
Create quite a din.

We can now see the caves
Kerrie, they're called.
Wish you were here
On this island of love.

Cheryl Campbell

YORK MINSTER

Whether you're a pilgrim or a tourist
York Minster is the place to be.
On a clear day climb the spiral stairs right to the top
And see the view for miles.
Then after you climb down
Take in the beauty and history of this cathedral.

E Bevans

The (Front) Garden Of England

Open plan;
Neatly fenced perhaps;
Or fortified against invasion.
Partly paved;
Hedged around for privacy;
Colourfully bordered, such a joy to see.

Is this Kent
The garden of the front of England's green and pleasant land?
Never bland;
Under pressure, yes, but still with space.
A special place of lowland, weald and marsh extending to the coast;
Rivers, cliffs and always room enough to boast
Of apples, hops and other fields which feed so many out of
their abundant yield.

Bob White

To Mickey

Many years ago, drawn in pen and ink,
Your antics had children laughing in glee,
A little black mouse in trousers of pink,
Together with a girlfriend called Minnie.
Now you draw to your huge Magic Kingdom,
Created by the imagination
Of a worldwide industry worth billions,
Holidaymakers from every nation.
Technology has teamed with fantasy,
Cartoon figures with creatures from all climes,
Children filled with marvel and ecstasy
At meeting characters from nursery rhymes!
From that little mouse in a quick cartoon,
Walt's expectation jumped over the moon!

Pat Heppel

Summer Sickness

A clutch of sunflowers
in a teapot makes me weep
for Aix-en Provence,

nostalgia growing
like the honey lavender
purpling the Vaucluse.

Norman Bissett

SNOWFALL SONNET

'Twas a crisp evening, sky covered with haze
Creatures hibernate away stirring days
Nightfall begins, the blanket starts to break
Falling star from above, spinning snowflake

Weeping silver snow on a winter's night
Icy angel tears frozen pearly-white
Broken glass crunches underfoot, sweet frost
Crystallised sparkle, world beneath is lost

Angels of winter, spray sugar around
Watching fairy lights fall straight to the ground
Frosty cotton sheet forming on the Earth
For children of the morn to show its worth

Happy faces, a Jack Frost creation
Winter snow, a Christmas decoration.

Nicola Steel

BIBURY

Deep, peaceful, slow,
The waters flow
At Bibury.

The lazy trout, suspended, dream
In the gently flowing stream
At Bibury.

The ducks, in many a friendly scuffle,
The surface of the waters ruffle
At Bibury.

Wee, crooked houses climb the hill
And time stands still
At Bibury.

Muriel Rawson

ROMAN KALEIDOSCOPE: LOST IN THE CITY STREETS OF ROME

Destination, Rome, empire of legend and history;
A place where time melts like destabilised toffee.
'Twas archaeological heaven, so onwards we hest,
Peeling back the layers of the past with our gladiatorial best.

First stop, the Pantheon - revered, stately, otherworldly;
Compared to St Peter's, more dignified, more godly.
The Renaissance riches of the Vatican, the tapestried halls;
Is the ancient word of Jesus lost 'midst the gold gilded walls?

Next, we marvelled at the old Forum where time stretched out
before us.
In contrast to *passeggiata;* new Rome gesticulating its chorus.
Blood of slave cruelty in Colosseo's skeletal heart;
Peaceful revellers at the Steps Espagñol trading stories until dark.

At night-time, in the back streets the spirits of yesteryear,
Flitted about us, tendering their unfulfilled ware:
Michelangelo painting twilight, ethereal and breathtaking,
Before darkness washed over it - the arrival of Caesar: King.

Black eclipse; Nero, fire, the gallop of chariots,
Spaghetti, wine, candlelight; checked bistro tablecloths.
While the old despot fiddles ash falls like mosaic flames;
Help, time's collapsing around us in Vesuvian waves . . .

Mark Anthony's *Rostra* - Cicero's head put on show.
Mopeds screech through red lights along the hazy, hairpin roads.
The crowd roars; it's deafening, but is it Stadio Olimpico or
Circus Maximus?
We're spinning with confusion - past or future through the
Arch of Janus?

Quick, throw a coin into the Trevi; stop this unruly mishmash,
Melee of spectre and extant, like Paul's road to Damascus.
A rich, ghostly, live history, old and new wrestling for throne.
All life here is eternal: All roads lead to Rome.

Carly Dugmore

Isle Of Wight

IOW what does that spell?
A fantasy world for me to tell
When once a child on holiday
IOW was a wonderful place to stay
Nothing's changed, not a grain of sand
Walks along the beach holding hands
IOW magic in a magical place
Always at a slower pace
A raw newness every day
Like your first trip round the bay
Childhood times I remember well
Time to share IOW's magic spell
Sleepy hollow of a place
This will do me, forever
How happy my man and me
Isle of Wight, meant to be!

Janet Hopkins

THE LAKE DISTRICT

The place I adore,
Is not where the sun sparkles upon the sea
Or the sand is golden.

The place I adore,
Is not where the boys are cute
Or the sky is a magnificent sea.

The place I adore,
Is pure beauty, it's where the grounds are green.
It's where the mountains disappear through the darkened sky.

The place I adore,
Is where clouds hang low and heavy
It's where there is the freshness of rain.

Amy Herbert (14)

THE WINTER GLOAMING

Grey clouds framed by a golden sky
Which shades to palest blue
Hold promise of more snow foreby
To coat the trees anew.
The gloaming, clear and cold and still
Becalms a winter's day
And frames the sheep upon the hill
As they flock 'round bales of hay
Fresh spread by callused, frozen hands
With fingertips so numb -
The shepherd, cursing snowbound land
As he longs for springtime sun.
Yet as he yearns for days to come
And his lifetime slips away
The gloaming darkens into night
'Til frost and stars hold sway.

Brian Beveridge

WINTER SEASON

W winter white
I ink-like nights
N naked trees
T temperatures freeze
E early to bed
R rest your head

S spring approaches
E end of winter reproaches
A aspirations
S snowy season
O omnipresence
N night-time essence.

Marian Bythell

Brighton Holiday

I'm on my holiday
Beside the sea
Looking outside
While I drink my tea.

The sea looks cold
The sky is grey
I wonder what
I will do today?

Shall I go to the shops
Or down to the pier
Or maybe the pub
And drink some beer?

Why has the sun
Decided to hide
Making the people
Stay inside?

I want to swim
And lay on the beach
I think next year
I will go to Crete!

Linda Leech

BURY MY HEART ON RHOSSILI BAY

Bury my heart on Rhossili Bay
Betwixt Burry Holms and Wild Worm's Head
Where the sunsets take your breath away
Dramatically turning the ocean red.
Bury my heart on Rhossili Bay
Where, when the wind howls I imagine it to be
The lament of sailors who have passed away
On stormy days in this cold, cruel bay.

Bury my heart on Rhossili Bay
Where the wreck of the Helvetia lies
And up Worm's Head furious waves spray
Under vast and mutable skies.
I've trod on the soil of lands far away
But nothing compares to Rhossili Bay.

Guy Fletcher

KENMORE ON LOCH TAY

My favourite place in all the world
Has got to be Kenmore.
It nestles in a quiet spot
On mighty Loch Tay's shore.
In Perthshire's glorious scenery
It takes its rightful place,
As one of Scotland's hideaways,
Where you can be at peace.

On Loch Tayside the Crannog stands,
Iron Age reconstruction,
It must have been some place to live
And now a grand attraction.
There's golf and fishing, boating too,
Outdoor pursuits in plenty,
And at Croft Na Caber take your pick
Of water sports wild or gently.

Our boat the *Shady Lady* stays
All summer at the 'Croft',
We come as often as we can
To sail around the Loch.
It always makes us feel at ease
And worries fade away,
When spending even just an hour
On beautiful Loch Tay.

Joan E Milne

Beautiful Kefalonia

Holidays are meant for fun
Relaxation in the sun
Drink the wine and taste the food
Feel the sunshine change your mood
Nurture love, don't spare expense
Seek out nature's every sense
Store up memories in the mind
Precious times you'll always find
You'll recall when old age binds
All you've cherished, all that's kind.

Barbara Harrison

STEP BACK IN TIME

Step back in time on the Isle of Wight
With meadows and acres of down
Round every corner are tempting sights,
Thatched villages abound.

Seventy miles of coastline
To walk, to cycle or ride,
Just while away your time
In this old-fashioned countryside.

Red squirrels you will see
Plus ospreys, adders and storks,
And delighted you will be
Whilst on these island walks.

This tropical island's frost-free,
The best climate in Great Britain,
With golden sands and sea
Which keeps many of us smitten!

Philippa Howard

MAY-BLETHORPE

It is, now and then, a dropped, broken ice cream cone
And melting vanilla smeared over the footpath.
Sea front shops and stalls are now displaying their own
Enticing wares. Glass encased clowns laugh.
Then, newly-sold beach balls with coloured segments fly
Either way over groynes nearly tennis-net high.

It is, very amateur rowers' arrhythmic
Oar-thumps on Queen's Park Lake. They give wild ducks (and geese)
A rather disturbed swim. The shock's nearly seismic -
So they waddle out in despair of any peace!
It is, precious vacant patches on the beach
Going spare, till they're claimed by a snazzy bath towel each.

Gillian Fisher

Where I Live

I used to live in Newport until they knocked our house down
Now I live in Rogerstone just outside of town
And here in my flat I am happy as can be
With a radio and TV for company
And in the winter my garden is covered in snow
But in the summertime lovely flowers will grow
Now to go to town I have to get a bus
And if it's late I try hard not to make a fuss
As I am always glad to get back home again
Even if it is sunny or if it should rain
As once I've locked my door and shut my windows tight
I know everything is going to be all right.

Eileen Kyte

YOSEMITE TRIP

The green tortoise rolls
Between these giant redwoods
Bearing warning alerts everywhere

Plugging on a bottle we huddle about
Others hide in bushes smoking pot as NY's son sleeps
And by the morning blueberry pancakes and BO

So we pack and undo the mechanical miracle
Turning our night caves into seats
Ready to roll through paper-caged bears.

Charles Jason Lee

EDEN?

I've found a little place at the bottom of our street
A temporal anomaly where worlds in parallel meet.
I keep the key safely, where no one else can find
It's hidden in a recess in the depths of my mind.
The first time that I went there, I couldn't believe what I saw
It's a place of flagrant green in a time of dinosaurs.
I have walked with the herds, roved across the land
Never seen a sign or hint of the existence of man.
So it's either in the future and we were never there
Or in the past before our time, but I just don't really care.
For I have seen the dinosaurs in all their splendid might
Seen moving herds extending far beyond my sight.
I can hear them calling in a world of different sound
I'm sure that they are talking as they leisurely move around.
I don't know if they see me, they don't bother if they do
Perhaps I'm so small and puny, they don't believe I'm true.
If ever there was an Eden, green and full and sweet
I think that I have found it in an anomaly down our street.

Terry Ireland

PARADISE

Eden revisited in glorious South Devon
with the scent of flowers that mingle
for hours, where lambs on the hillside
frolic about to the bird's song and
the bees hum all the day long.
Sunshine carpets each blade of grass
where daisies and buttercups spring
while a wispy white cloud under a
pure blue sky is the reason to
enthral one to sing.
The tall silver birch trees with branches
that span upwards and outwards as if to
scan the sun's summer glow, caressing each
leaf that create intricate patterns
as I lie here beneath.
As evening approaches, the sun is sublime
and sends down rays like the touch of a wand,
the shrubs in the shade of the
silver birch trees are now steeped
in gold and serenity.

Hazel Sheppard

Welcome To Chapel-En-Le-Frith

'C apital of the Peak' its claim to fame,
H ills that encompass, like green embossed frame.
A town that has grown round small forest church,
P lenty to find when you start to search.
E lements of days of so long ago,
L inger awhile as you glance to and fro.

E ach of the inns with a history to tell,
N or heedless of houses, grand halls as well.

L anes that are narrow for you to explore,
E verywhere secrets just lying in store.

F ollow the signposts to our market place,
R ecall distant past each sight does embrace.
I f to the old hearse house you then proceed,
T here maps, guides and handbooks, all you could need.
H oping sincerely you'll return with great speed, and
wishing you well, where'er your paths lead.

Trish Lomas

THE SWAN

How elegant and beautiful you are to me,
You can fly in the sky and set yourself free.
You can swim on the lake, watch the trees pass you by,
The perfect creation which brings tears to my eye.

Your feathers are the most brightest of white,
Just like angels wings, the most purest light.
So soft and secure just like Heaven above,
Precious and wise, you bring divine love.

Jacqueline Ann Ralph

MY GARDEN

A piece of earth with shrubs and trees
With perfumed flowers and honeybees.

Where songbirds sing their song of love
With nightingale and turtle dove.

When winter comes, the north wind blows
The flowers gone from bush and rose.

All living things are out of sight
No creature braves the ice-cold night.

But with spring there is rebirth
And beauty paints this piece of Earth.

And when the summer sun shines through
The colours are of every hue.

I would not part for any price
With this, my land, my paradise.

Denise Castellani

TREASURE

As the summer season comes around,
There are bounteous treasures to be found.

A spider's web in the morning dew,
The rainbow-coloured mist you can see right through.

Hot white sun riding in the sky,
The old oak tree lending shade nearby,
Shimmering shades of summer heat
Finds the moist green frog in his pond, replete.

Hover flies and bumblebees
Fanning their wings in the warm west breeze.

Mosaic patterns in the mixed flower border,
Give a sparkling riot of bright disorder.
A stunning drift of Lavandula,
Jewel bright flowers of splashing colour.

Heady smell of night-scented sky,
Birds asleep in branches high.
Night pierced to the heart by dawn's first ray,
Sky-pink, green and gold, at the break of the day.

To the summer season nature brings
The diversity of all these things.

D M Ellis

MOTHER NATURE'S THERAPY

I love to see the moon so bright
With stars that twinkle through the night
Against a sky that is so dark -
The contrast fills me with delight.

Then at dawn, I like to view
The moors and hills around us too,
Their smooth contours, green with trees,
Are features that will always please.

Lower down, through grassy slopes,
A tinkling stream runs by,
Its ripples glitter in the sun
That brightly shines on high.

Brilliant also is the sky:
A rich blue hue now delights the eye.

Scenes such as these help us unwind -
And if some folk were not so blind,
They too would find true peace of mind
From nature's gift to all mankind.

Francis Hodgkinson

PAST PARTICIPANTS

That day his shop -
fruit and veg, competitive prices -
was destroyed by lava
from Vesuvius,
together with the baths,
where later he'd have met his friends,
the bar where that night they'd have
sunk a few pints,
Oh and, of course, he himself
and all of them.

And today I stood there
in his shop, at his counter,
wandered, hot and tired through
the shattered Town Baths,
the ornate little bars
and heard an anonymous voice
through the hired audio guide
speculating on what
daily life was like
in his Pompeii.

There were no ghosts there, of course,
amid such a plethora of tourists.
But, in his own little shop, perhaps
an impression in the air,
the hint of a greeting
across the
intervening centuries.

Celia Andrews

CORNISH CREAM

Dreams of Eden,
Lost gardens,
Hidden valleys,
All foundered on Atlantic lows,
As misty rain throws
Unrelenting,
Sweeping through the coves,
Splattering the running panes.
June raining
Not flaming,
To dampen Cornish dreams.
But next day!
Lows chased away,
A high
With sky of brilliant blue,
Atlantic green,
Sparkles in the coves.
Eden filled with droves
And gardens found, valleys seen,
The richest Cornish cream.

Pat Ladbrooke

Penang: Pearl Of The Orient

The sea hawks are drifting over the harbour
Sharp eyes ready for that flash of silver,
See the fisherman in his small boat
Chugging bravely into the Straits of Malacca
Dodging the pirates.

Look past the tall, glass covered buildings, neon in the night,
The markets, the shophouses where I played as a child:
Talking to Ali, next door, making chapattis.
Going to the sweetshop, five cents for polar mints
Twenty cents for dried sour plums and red ginger.

Rise up, rise into the clouds and jungle,
The secret heart of the island,
The mossy branches and great roots loom in the half-light.
Tree branches whip back and forth
From tribes of monkeys playing where they reach for the sun.
The air hums with the high keening of small wings,
Find deep pools where truant boys played on ropes.

Tall pagodas filled with incense,
Minarets of the crescent moon
Calling to prayer.
The high winds curl the waves
On the lazy beaches,
Casuarina and coconut dance their waltz:
The pine's dark skirts sweeping the silver sand,
The palm's slim trunk extending a coaxing hand.

Pey Colborne

KINGS PORT

Doesn't it just make you feel so proud?
Want to jump up and scream out loud!
Like victorious chants from the Anfield crowds?
The Liver-birds are our Culture vultures.

We took on the best and beat them all,
like when Adolph sent his bombers, we answered the call.
Odds stacked against us, but we all stood tall,
now we're going to be the *Capital Of Culture.*

Take a ferry across the Mersey, Gerry's home base,
gallop up to Aintree for the National race.
Our George and John's memories are all over the place,
And Doddy's still the master of fools.

The architecture here is a must to be seen,
multicultural city, cosmopolitan cuisine.
Kingsway tunnel, opened by Elizabeth, the Queen,
the tall ships heading back to the 'Pool.

Jimmy McGovern, Alan Bleasdale, Willy Russel and me,
grab a pad and a pen, and switch off the TV.
Face a blank page wondering what it will be,
and write long and deep into the night.

You can reach us by train, by sea, or by air,
we're the people with the magic, you'll find everywhere,
and thanks to the Mancs' for supporting us there,
now our waterfront's a World Heritage site.

Thomas Francis Sean McBride

A Cornish Dream

The wonderful views across Cornwall's coast,
Cliff-top walks across the rugged coastline,
The deep blue sea with big white chargers
That lash against the rocks,
Perfect surfers' paradise,
Always something new to be explored,
The air is fresh and clear,
History is all around us here,
Part of England's heritage,
A special retreat,
For Cornwall's tourists,
A special treat.

L Kelley

BLACKPOOL

We went to Blackpool to see the lights
Illuminations, what a lovely sight.
The Tower stood out all bright and bold
A few years ago it was painted gold.
The Tower Ballroom you can sit and admire
The Wurlitzer playing tunes you can
Listen to and not tire.
For as many hours as you like to linger
There is no need to have a singer.
Looking up at the ornate ceilings from the floor below
The lights from the chandeliers are all aglow.
Couples dancing to their own style
To leave all life's troubles behind for a while.

Marian Clark

Market Harborough

Market Harborough in Leicestershire
Is a favourite town for me.
People come from far and near
For there's such a lot to see.
Robert Smyth's Grammar School (1614) still stands there.
Since twelve hundred under stout oak legs.
Long ago, local folk to sell their fare
Brought fresh butter, fresh cheese and fresh eggs.
The Church of St Dionysius is close by,
Its broad spire the best in the land.
By rippling water wildlife you'll espy
On riverside walk near at hand.
High Street is bright, good buildings abound.
There's 'Three Swans' proud, wrought iron sign,
And the Old Town Hall when you're looking around,
Much to admire in a borough so fine.
On New Canal basin narrowboats rest.
In the clear air one feels happy and free.
P'raps on reflection which town you like best
Hope Market Harborough your first choice will be.

Loré Föst

AUTUMN POEM

Autumn is a happy time,
with the wind rushing through the trees,
just close your eyes and listen
to gentle sounds upon the breeze.

Later in the season,
the leaves turn ruby-red,
falling to the ground below,
where hedgehogs make their beds.

Even later on you'll see
mist rising in the morn,
look outside your window
upon nature's wonderful dawn.

So as this season's ending,
another will begin,
wrap up nice and warm now,
as winter's chill sets in.

Sarah Grantham

MERANO

Let me take you to Merano, up in the South Tyrol
A mixture of Austria and Italy, its charm and beauty will enthral
Snow-capped mountains in the distance, flowers and palm trees in the town
The fast-flowing Passirio river comes rushing and tumbling down
From here you can visit the Dolomites, or take a trip down to Lake Garda
Ride cable-cars in the mountains, so many different paths to wander
Stroll leisurely by the river, in sunshine or in shade
See the rainbow colours of the flowers that never seem to fade
And if you happen to like music, then this is the place for you
From classical to jazz, bands and easy listening too
And as you take your evening stroll, you might hear music from afar
And perhaps you'll enjoy a concert sat beneath the moon and stars
Soon I will be lured back because I've fallen under its spell
I love its elegance and ambience, I'm smitten, can't you tell?
And when I return I'll feel at home and enjoy it for all it's worth
In Merano I have truly found a piece of Heaven on Earth.

Carolyn Jones

From A Caravan Club CL Site, Cold Ashby Northants

Early morning
Mid August,
From the camper window a tranquil scene.
The rose of the shires, Northants,
High up here, lush, verdant in full summer green.

Falling away
Gently, gradually
On either side a patchwork land
Of fields and hedgerows, they roll
Then rise again to distant wooded hills, a dim blue band.

The A14
A lazy hum
Enhancing the stillness, the solitude, the peace.
Moving slowly, cropping grass
In the next field, sheep, black faces, white fleece.

A mistle thrush
Speckled breast
Feeds on berries red on laden rowan trees,
While among the sheep a loping hare
Stops, sits up and for a moment seems to freeze.

A fine day promised
Deep blue sky
Stray cotton wool clouds, gentle breeze stirs ash and lime
Almost another world, in its quietness
There seems to be a pausing, a stepping out of time.

Frances Marie Cecelia Harvey

Loch Ness

The deep dark waters
guarded by green, wooded mountains,
keep their secrets safe.

Beneath the serene surface
lurk history and mystery,
myth and legend,
life both natural and supernatural,
real and imagined.

Matt Ebeling

ST MICHAEL'S MOUNT

A forest was submerged by sea
Fifteen hundred years before Pytheas
Came here in three-two-five BC

This way came prehistoric men,
Brought with them Irish copper, gold
Much tin to Gaul was shipped out then

Great Vision of the Guarded Mount
Seen by fishermen in four-nine-five AD
John Milton's Lycidas gave the account

St Michael the Archangel's name
For Ictis the small isle near Belerion
St Michael's Mount in time became

A fortress, priory church and home
Such beauty, grandeur, history here to see
And climb the Mount still pilgrims come

By sea a forest now submerged
Bare feet and wheels traverse a causeway just
Until in mighty power the sea's re-surged

Such awesome power, the sea is master still
And Ictis ever subject to its will

Enid Gill

AUNTY ADELE'S ANEMONES

Across the meadow green,
As we passed away the hours,
We came across a beautiful scene
Of brightly coloured flowers.
I asked, 'What beautiful flowers are these
Which we're not allowed to touch?'
'They're Aunty Adele's anemones,
She sells them by the bunch.'
We carried on and made our way towards the giant tree,
Climbed as far as we could reach
And looked out towards the sea.

J Hagen

PARADISE

A wonderful place, where I was at ease,
Listening to the palms rustle, in the tender breeze,
A delicate scent passing under my nose
Of whispering seas and salty shallows,
The golden-white sand trickling through my toes
Here in paradise where time just froze,
The beautiful flowers and the fruits from the trees
So pure and so beautiful, just hard to believe,
Where I saw a shade much deeper than green
The rainforest foliage just had to be seen,
And now as we lie here on the quiet dark beach
Searching the skies on the magical reef,
A sparkling flash quite beyond our belief
A shooting star passed as we lay beneath,
Now here in this place our hearts will always belong
Where the people all smile and the living is long,
Paradise we found in this St Lucian isle,
Tucked in the Caribbean, where time stood still for a while.

Sarah Colquitt

THE CITY THAT NEVER SLEEPS

I find the one place to be
is New York city,
from the subway to Madison Square,
or in amongst the nitty gritty,
travel down to downtown or up,
to Broadway or Empire State,
or any coffee shop,
the tri-state is filled with life,
small boutiques, tenements,
the blue and white,
patrol from Upper East Side,
to 24th and fifth,
Sinatra sang the songs,
across the Brooklyn Bridge,
shopping at Macys,
skating in the park,
donut shops and hot dog stands,
are all in my heart,
got caught between the moon
and New York city,
from the first point at JFK,
to the skyline so pretty,
took a Greyhound,
on the Hudson River line,
spent time in Times Square,
it's all in my mind,
Lady Liberty tells me it's easy to remember,
that the buildings may have changed since the 11th of September,
but the New Yorkers living in 'New York, New York'
still live the life, talk the talk, and always walk the walk.

Antony Hammond

HOLIDAY AFFAIR

(Dedicated to T J And AJ)

Sand between my toes
Golden in the sun
Away with all my woes
A new affair has begun
Paradise by the moonlight
Gentle breeze upon my skin
I could die to only hold tight
What my soul does feel within
Whispering to your wave
You soothe my every sense
Calming this city so brave
Creating my innocence
I love you, I honestly do
If only we'd last forever
Nobody matters but you
I treasure each moment together
For when all my lovers do disappear
And I'm nursing a heart so broken
I can always hold you near
Never to judge, remain, unspoken
So my ocean I just need to thank you
For always being there
Always open, honest and true
I could never holiday anywhere
But here with you

Claire Valentine

SOLAR SOLACE

I'm in the sun, I know he is there
Though my senses betray me, I welcome his fare
I simply can't touch him or hear his worth
His existence I cannot determine by taste
While nostrils may swell, he escapes even smell
By sight I see shadows, I know all too well

But his fiery face in the sky
Is outwith the reach of the unsheltered eye
Aware of your presence though not by sight or will
Behind my closed eyes, my head with light is filled

For poor man and rich man your bounty is free
Warm golden orb, you bring the primitive to knee
Welcoming light at the east sign of dawn
Till your arc is completed and is westering gone

Unmeasured pleasure absorbed in the rays
Filtered honey, be nature's kiss
Countless treasured hours of idyllic days
Groweth the green wonder of photosynthesis

Patrick Martin

SANDCASTLES

Wispy clouds of white, like cotton balls,
glide silently across a light blue sky . . .
The wind strong, cool, and yet still lazy,
creates rippled white-capped waves . . .
Dancing o'er a bluish-green ocean,
gently falling onto the foreshore . . .
Footprints, meander across a sandy beach,
to no particular destination . . .
The rising tide, now gently erasing all signs
of man's invasion . . .
Gulls soar and dive on thermals high,
the lazy wind beneath their wings . . .
Seashells scattered across the sands,
spread like seeds of corn . . .
Broken sandcastles, from children's play,
an endearing sight on this sandy glade.

Nicholas Maughan

BLACK CLOUD

Steady with the journey onward
Now wiser
Seeing with unclear but determined vision
Mind fully ready for the possibility
Ready to see the friendly face of death
Body in waiting
Expectant
Waiting for it to strike
Watch the hills
For the rolling black cloud
Heavy with rain
How long till the storm?
How soon till the sun breaks through?

Sara Pyefinch

THE SUPREME GARDENER

Our greenhouse is bursting with baby plants,
Protected from inclement weather,
The season is right, just turning late spring,
Entering early summer.

The garden is ready, cultivated and dug,
Given nutrients and hoed with a fervour,
Added to this much patience and love,
Poured out in equal measure.

Flowers are planted in their home at last,
To delight us with radiant hue,
The bees and the birds will do all they can,
Cross pollinate colours new.

We can propagate, germinate,
Use all our skills, to eliminate every weeds,
But we wouldn't have our gardens today,
If God hadn't first made the seed.

Dorothy M Mitchell

FLOWERS ON A BLACK FROST DAY

Flowers on a black frost day;
A morn so crisp,
That you might break off a piece of sun
And suck on it like barley sugar.
Swallows in the midst of winter.
Air so pure
It could be bottled up
And used to cure despairing patients,
Or anyone whose shadow
Looms larger than themselves.
Suppressing clouds . . .
That rain champagne.

Cobwebs bejewelled in drops of dew
That entrap light like a chandelier.
A sunset that lasts a thousand years.

Fishing boats upon a moonlit tide.
Shells whipped up in ice cream waves,
And thrown onto the shore as gifts.
Stars that romance the loneliest of nights,
Stencilled onto a purple sky.

Samantha Crossley

Inspired By Nature

The sun always comes o'er the sea
And bathes all the land in a glow
Then past hill and plain to the Cheviot
From the sea to the west, flow and go, flow and go.

This land of cliff, moor and castle
I'll never tire of, that there's no chance
No Blackpool or London is this land
Tranquil and peaceful, so filled with romance.

Landscapes of tradition and splendour
The links with the past plain to see
Huge castles like Bamburgh and Alnwick
All through strife and war, it's now free.

The living past is still thriving
Embodied in Cragside so grand,
One's eyes open wide in amazement
Wherever one goes in this land.

Ralph Littlewood

COUNTRYSIDE

Where and when a flowering plant will be found,
Will be determined by a combination of sounds.

The type of soil, the amount of light and shade,
Temperature, rainfall, and shelter from the wind,
Are all important to the well-being of the plant,
Being in the light or shade.

As you grow in experience, you will soon discover
That you can make a good guess at the type of plants
Likely to be found in an area, just by looking at the plant
Knowing your experience.

Most plants in the countryside, like orchids,
Prefer the alkaline soil that forms over chalk and limestone soil,
But the heathers prefer the acid soil.

You will need very little in the way of equipment
If you want to go out flower-hunting,
A notebook and identification guide is all you need
For plant-hunting

When you go out to look for plants, always take a notebook,
Sketch any plants you see into a notebook.
Sketch any plants you cannot identify on the spot,
And include a description of the leaves as well as the flowers,
And look at the leaves, this too into a notebook.

Remember, draw the plant, do not pick the plant,
Do not pick it; if you can't draw the plant
Take photographs of the plant,
Every flower picked means fewer seeds to
Begin the next generation of plants.

Leave the plants for someone else to enjoy later.
Save the plants.

Paulette Coulter

A Walk Through The Woods In January

Dripping softly through the trees
Chains of droplets sparkle here,
Cascading one by one from view.

The wood is beautiful these days.
The trees soar up arranged against a bright sky
And wood birds strut and sing.
Now I see the slippery bark
Blue-grey with lichen
Furry with age-old moss, like comfy breeches
Hugging the old stumps.

Leaves are dotted through the dark
Like luminescent copper.
No summer this though -
But bountiful winter,
With visions of beyond through bare branches
Tipped with buds ready to burst,
Long before decay of leaf.

No sadness here, no dreary gloom
Alive, alive is winter's wood
Filled with the promise not of spring,
But of this season's rare delight.

And all along the crunchy track
The leathery leaves of holly
Snuggle beside the ruby stems of dogwood
Warm and willowy.
And fuzzy shapes of ivy rise
To climb the knobbly trunks -
Just here and there.

A watery beam of sun catches a particle of water
Sitting on a leaf -
Just here and there.
And all around the trees are not quite waiting
Alive, alive is winter's wood.

Karen Lewis

THE WAVES

As I stand on the rocks
I look towards the sea
The waves building up
Their short lives
They build up and crash down
I stand there and realise that our lives are not much different
They are the same
We are born and we die
Just like a wave
Some waves die down gently
And some crash down
Maybe that's how we decide to die
We can give up
And die gently
Or we can put up a fight
And die in a blaze of glory
Which one would you choose?
I know which one I would choose
I have not lived these few years
On Earth just to die gently and give up
I have given a lot up in my life
And when it comes to my time
I am going to put up a fight
I will get my view across.

Anthony Crump

UNTITLED

Crows are all black
But baby crows are not
The difference between them is a lot
Baby crows are weak and small
But a big crow is strong and tall
A baby crow doesn't need much to stay alive
They only need a little to survive.

Anna Deeley (9)

Discount Day At The Garden Centre

Poppies and roses are blazing bright red,
Plants stand in long rows in pots of dark peat,
A white lily's face lies crushed and quite dead,
But people just queue, to drink and to eat.

Plants stand in long rows in pots of dark peat,
Radiant and bright, each sweet flower opens wide.
But people just queue, to drink and to eat,
The thriving new plants are pushed to one side.

Radiant and bright, each sweet flower opens wide,
Look at the colour, you dreary grey crowd.
The thriving new plants are pushed to one side,
Grown for spring sunshine now ready and proud.

Look at the colour, you dreary grey crowd,
A white lily's face lies crushed and quite dead.
Grown for spring sunshine, now ready and proud,
Poppies and roses are blazing bright red.

Sheila Culshaw

My Poem

Green grass sways in the gentle breeze,
Trees stand tall making sure everything is in place.
Roads run away as if scared by the tranquillity.
A wooden bridge arches over a rushing river,
Letting people trample on it as they please.
Horses swat at passing flies, as they doze in the midday sun.

Leaves fall from the tall oak trees, making a golden path.
The sun arrives late, keeping the golden land dark.
Animals start to go to sleep till the end of the winter.

Winter is here now, grey, cold winter.
Paths are sludgy, and the river cold.
But however cold, this place stays beautiful.

Benjamin White (11)

JESTER OF THE WOODS

The drumming of the oak's tattoo
Although unseen, I know it's you,
With crimson mask and jewelled eye
The jester of the woods is sly,
A lightning flash of green and gold
His character is not so bold,
Heard, not seen, a laughing cry
Who does he mock, and why?
There! With creeping reptile grace
The joker now reveals his place,
Elusive though he may have been
The joke's on him, for he was seen.

Mark L Moulds

You Know Me Well

I am warm and sunny,
and make light of the spirit;
I caress barley fields,
and make a moving sea of silk;
I turn trees into nature's windchimes,
And make dreams fly on the -
horizon of clouds;
I incense you with scents,
of flora and fauna,
and make your soul dance -
with joy;
And like I,
you would have wings for some -
days of a season;
You know me well,
I am summer's breeze.

Amanda Kitching

The River

Softly, silently, runs the river,
Twisting, turning toward the sea.
Beneath its waters so crystal clear
Swim the fishes, on a merry spree.
Along its banks, the otters preside,
Watching with interest as small boats glide.
The willow tree hangs low and weeping,
The angler, his watch is keeping.
When night falls and moon is glowing,
The waters are likened to a lady's gown,
Of silver, shimmering and flowing.
Sparkles as of sequins show,
As ripples do their dancing to and fro.
A sudden swish disturbs the still
As water rat hunts for a kill.
What secrets deep dark water holds?
Those only know within its folds.

Edna Freeland

It Rains In Africa

There are dry tees
And orange leaves
The warmth of the sun
The coolness of the breeze
The smell of the sand
A marriage of moist and dust
Embracing my nostrils
Quenching my thirst for change.
Shadows of flying birds
Reflect on bowers
Across the bluest
Skies at midday.
It rains in Africa
Children are playing
Under the heavy downpour
With no worries of asthma or 'flu
The commissioner sips hot tea
With his family
Our neighbours are all
Wrapped up in bed
My friends watch the TV
But I stand alone
Looking out through the window
Watching the rain as it falls.

Kifayah AbdulQuadri

A Beginning

Bury me deep away from frost,
In the earth so warm and kind
Nurture, care for me at all cost
I will grow when I've a mind.

One small seed, perfectly formed
So fragile and yet so strong
The sun burns down and I am warmed
Be patient, I'll not be too long.

My roots are locked into the ground
And I'm feeling motivated
Some urgency to emerge I've found
My shoots are elevated.

I strive to reach up to the sky
As my top is duly crowned
With flowering blooms, by and by
Dancing, without making a sound.

Do not pick me; please let me be
For as long as I can survive
Leave me for everyone to see
Beautifully scented, alive.

Doreen Fillary

THE ENDEARING BEAUTY OF NATURE

Sometimes I sit and listen to the sounds of the tranquil sea.
I sit and watch the sun glint off thc golden beach.
I look to my right and see the perfectly formed harbour,
And watch the small fishing boats bob up and down upon its waters.

I get up and walk down off the sand dunes
I transgress over the bridge and make my way down to the small river.
It makes a slow gurgling noise as it travels back past me.
The further along beside it I go, the more wooded the area becomes.

The view above becomes littered with overhanging branches.
Occasionally a shard of light bursts through, uncovering the path.
I find a bench and rest, I look around at what is there.
I see the red berries on trees and I hear the calls of birds.

These things I see and hear
Are all forms of natural beauty,
But in these days and times, sadly
There are only few who still appreciate them.

Chris Brewer

Spring

Winter's quickly slipping by, soon it will be spring
When the trees burst into bud, and all the birds do sing.
Crocuses and daffodils with their colourful display
Help brighten up the saddest heart, and like a carpet lay
Of orange, mauve and yellow and white among the green.
What a pretty picture! What a pretty scene!
For nature's such a wondrous thing, as the seasons come and go,
We're always blessed with something good, for the Lord God
makes it so.

M Weavers

Summer

When soft, warm winds are swaying
the heaving, bursting rose buds
and fork-tailed busy martins
build their nests of mud.

When woodlands dress in green attire
to clothe their boughs, once bare,
and nature's tuneful symphony
of birdsong fills the air.

Pointed-petalled celandines
reflect the sun's gold face,
while in the shade, the ferns uncoil
their fronds, like fans of lace.

When cows graze in the meadows
and hedgerows overgrown,
ripe berries, plump and juicy spurt,
elder, rosehip, sloe.

The pungent smell of mown grass
wafting on summer breeze,
butterflies and dragonflies
and humming bumblebees.

Midday sun rays cast a sheen
upon the silver lake,
teal and shelducks glide along
their babies in their wake.

When barley in the fields grows high,
red poppies peer between,
the countryside in summer time
is peaceful and serene.

Pandy Pond

GAIETY

The gayest songs of the morning
As the mist climbs over the hills,
For they dance and they dance in the eastern world
While humanity pays its bills.
For the song of the moonlight sonata
And the frost on the snow-white fields
Oh they dance, and they dance in the eastern world
While the yellow harvest yields.
And they dance and they dance in the eastern world
The gayest songs of the morning.

Peter Buss

QUARRY AT MACHYNLLETH

Deep in the quarry's bottom,
In a hole rent by man's desire to build,
Mother Earth has reclaimed her space.
Green, lush and luxurious,
In the damp mid-March.
Rising high; sheets of sheer slate.
The ground; verdant, moss-strewn,
Where once a stream flowed.
A life-giving space,
Where once there was none.
With trees, mosses and ferns.
Moss covering slate and trees,
Life on life,
Trees of green,
With moss dangling from branches like catkins.
Decaying branches supporting life; giving life,
In nature's never-ending cycle.
Life-giving water, sheeting down rock,
The dripping of water,
The roaring of wind in the trees,
Creating a meditative sound,
In this peaceful, perfect place.

Alex Mylles

The Birds In December

It's strange to hear the birds' chorus in December:
squealing, squawking, screaming,
chirping, chattering, cawing, crowing,
twittering, tweeting; all this
echoing from all corners.
The sky is leaden, mist hangs over the sea
and rain is in the air.
But the birds continue,
in their element.

Jennifer Richards

A Boring Day

What a boring day!
People say.
The weather is cool
Birds in flight, flying
The sun's already vanished
Evening twilight glowing
Soft breeze blowing
People lie half-naked
In front of sea waves.

Children running
Parents chatting
Birds in flight, flying
What a boring day!
Children laughing
Parents smiling
Birds in flight chirruping
In the pure blue skies.

Bolaji St Ramos

INTERLUDE

Ice-blue skies, feathered red,
Tingling lips, cold and numb,
Silver moonbeams over the lake,
With joyous heart, I await
The beautiful swans to appear.

Necks poised high, they gracefully glide
As dancers, beneath the stars.
Plumage so sleek, porcelain-white.
No, I'm not dreaming.
A magical aura, sheer delight.

Diana Frewin

ERMINE AND FEATHERS

Swathes of rape seed flowers surround me where I laze,
A breeze caressing gently as they sway in golden haze.
The rising sun warms slowly, petals open as I gaze
And dewdrops on the flowers flash reflecting the sun's rays.

Towards the far horizon I see fields of brilliant blue
Where linseed blossoms melt into the sky of self-same hue
That's brushed with streaks of ermine or gull's feathers floating by
Which look at though they might just spiral earthwards where I lie.

Here, nature's patchwork pinafore enwraps me side to side,
Its pockets filled with gifts of beauty spreading far and wide.
I can forget my troubles, for a short time I can hide
From a world that's changed, and getting old, I can't keep up -
I've tried!

Paddy Jupp

ROSES

A bevy of beauties in one place
Which one to pick is up to you
Just take a look at each one's face
White ones, pink ones, red ones, blue.

The blue ones now, aren't so common
They're the rarest of the lot
But e'er so, though not so often
Someone hybrids them in a pot.

There e'en once was a black one
Now did you e'er see such a thing?
Again someone did have it done
And for that he was crowned king!

Such lovely girls in lovely robes
All crinoline, fluffy and gay
Upturned, showing bright petticoats
With wide enticing smiles all day.

They're debutantes - belles of the ball
Their cards are marked by eager bees
Who dance them round - one and all
No dance is left for you and me.

End of the day and their robes wilt
By morning dew they're puffed and faint
They shed brown dresses - no, no kilt
And by dusk you find them bent.

Liz Barnor

Falling Rain

I love to watch Earth drink
Of the water of the rain
I love to watch the green of the fields
As they gulp from Heaven's hand
I love to watch the fearless trees
As they dance gladly in misty wind
I love to watch the sky
As she pours down the rains
For little children's play.
I love to hear the thunder break
Over our roofs
I love to watch the excited ponds
Revive with the touch of nature's wand
I love to watch the flash of lightning
As she breaks the thunders loose
I love to watch the birds
As they pair and sing in shelter from the rain
I love to watch in silent words
The bliss of nature's bloom.
I love to watch your laughter
Your smiles that set my heart abeam.

Charles Okafor

BEAUTIFUL

The trees wave their branches as the wind weaves between
snowflake blossom; beautiful petals fall to the ground.
Birds wake their song at dawn and flit from fence to post
spying the early worm or maybe yesterday's toast
left by the little girl with beautiful blonde hair
who looks for the robin that visits them each year.
A friend of the garden, a beauty to observe
so watch the garden's beauty grow with the love it truly deserves.

Ali Newman

Country Life

The tolling of a distant bell
Echoing through this lovely dale
The songbirds' morning chorus, all is well
The early summer sun's warming rays

A glittering brook flows gently by
Trickling over well-worn stones
Grazing sheep on pastures high
Above these peaceful country roads

Chocolate-box cottages side by side
Their open windows invite the sun
Spirals of smoke from chimneys high
Another day has now begun

Country folk dressed in best apparel
As village life now starts to stir
Walk along to ancient chapel
They'll all join in their morning prayer

The passing of time's had little effect
Things are much the same as before
It's country life at its very best
In this tranquil place that I adore

Harry Murtagh

LINDISFARNE

There is no other place quite like it;
No atmosphere that can compare,
And yet there are castles elsewhere,
Other monasteries to visit,
Prettier harbours to be seen,
Sites with hidden treasures to be found.
But here there are secrets in store,
Ones sensed, rather than seen.
Faint echoes borne on the wind;
Resonating from yesterday
From all corners of the island
Falling on the ears of today.
Good and evil has been done
By good and evil visitors called,
Drawn by the same inner voice.
For where good resides,
Evil will seek it out
To meet it in battle.
The presence of the Sainted hermit
Lingers on the inner isle
With the same sense of serenity
That he found, and deposited
For use at a later date,
By all who would seek it out.
The causeway, a portcullis,
Raised and lowered by no-man's-hand.
Opens to all without favour,
But closes just as surely again.
Visions of bloody massacres
By marauding Viking hordes,
Stand alongside scenes of pious endeavour
By devoted monks and pilgrims.

There is an overwhelming sense
That an unsolved mystery still remains,
And the enlightened spirit will feel
The touch of the ‘unseen’ hand at work.

Bryan Davies

Relaxing Into Life

Looking into the world
Cycles of nature
Seen

Rhythm
Purpose

Beauty

Security

The sea always meets
The shore

Looking into the world
Crested flowing waves
Altered

Rhythm
Destroyed

Turmoil

Pain

The sea always vulnerable
To rocks

Looking into the world
Fears recognised as
Useless

The sea always meets
The shore

Regardless of the journey

Anabel Green

Waiting For Spring

Spring will surely come,
The daffodil will return.
The frost and snow will go,
And sun will make us warm.

Snowdrops are the first to shine,
Their sweet little bells give us hope.
'Tis a winter flower that is pure and sweet,
No longer look out of the window and mope.

The crocus follows and the daffodils tall,
Their golden trumpets tell us, spring is near.
And weary winter is on its way out,
Lengthening days fill us with cheer.

Enjoy the spring, 'tis Earth's rebirth,
Plan the things in summer that you wish to do.
Each day grows longer. Summer is near,
Make sure this blessing reaches you.

The lawn will look greener when it is cut,
And bedding plants will begin to cheer.
Your garden will respond to sunshine's bliss,
And the red geraniums will stand out clear.

Albert E Bird

WINTER IS APPROACHING

Winter is approaching quick and fast
With glistening streets and slippery paths,
The cold wind blows hoping it will bring snow
Gently falling from the sky,
Swirling and swaying as it goes by,
Pure new and clean as it clutches to the evergreen.

The fields are covered just like a white blanket.
On the fence a robin sits looking at rabbits
That are leaping and jumping and running quick,
Mother Nature has sent this from above,
So on with hats, scarves, gloves
And go and explore, just what's in store.

This wonderful magical season
Making snowmen and throwing snowballs,
Sliding down banks, having lots of tumbles.
Your hands get so cold
And your feet feel like ice
So watch where you tread
And always think twice.
The feeling of winter sends
Shivers down your spine,
Let's hope it comes back
Time after time.

Maddie Reade

A Day In The Life Of Summer

Seeing primrose
Smiling through
Misty comfort
Youthful dew
Singing heavens
Softly blue
Crystal clearly
Brightly new.

Dancing footprints
Weaving gold
Fluid journey
Jewel unfold.
Shining laughter
Rainbow shoal
Breathing nectar
Drinking soul.

Lightly waves
Watery moon
Starry sprinkled
Indigo room
Shifting gentle
Cloudy dune
Flavour purple
Night perfume.

Jacqui Fleming

WELCOME WINTER!

Who's knocking at the door?
It's Winter trying to get in to change the light,
the temperature and the feel of the place.
The house glowed with autumn light and colour.
Bowls were filled to the brim with late summer
fruits waiting to be preserved. Vases overflowed
with nasturtiums and geraniums with vivid intensity.
Carved pumpkin lanterns shone on the table.
Winter wants to change all that, and makes us
shiver and find our woolly jumpers.
But no! Let's keep him outside.
We'll close the door tightly so he can't invade the house.
The autumn colours may have blown away, and all may be
forlorn outside. But now cosiness comes creeping in.
Polishing the oak furniture vigorously will make us tingle
and give a sheen to mirror all the lights in the room.
A dish of rosy apples will lend perfume, and scarlet candles
will adorn the mantelpiece.
Mellow embers in the grate may toast the crumpets
for tea and then they'll drip with butter and honey.
Winter's cold will be melted and hearts and hearths
will throb with cheer. Welcome Winter!

Christine Lemon

FLURRIES OF LEAVES

Focus on the smell of the mountainside
Luxurious growth, and fast moving mists
And the sound of torrents down to the village below
Focus on the deep flooded quarry near the mountaintop
Scenic autumn abundance near the homes.

Michael C Soper

ODE TO BOGNOR REGIS

Hello Bognor! Busy little Georgian seaside town!
Holiday destination of my 1950's childhood.
Here I am again - and look at you now!

Within the modern town, the Arcade boasts its newly re-tiled towers
above the entrance to this earlier purveyor of retail pleasures
and farther round the promenade, The Royal Norfolk Hotel
sports its prominent colourful seal of royal approval
and spreads its multi-bedroomed arms in elegant welcome
from behind its discreet hedge-lined lawns and private frontage.

Bognor Regis - the first part of its name would seem to belie the last
but this place boasts a fashionable regal past
as evidenced by the elegant Georgian buildings of the Steyne:
its tight-packed terraced residences jostling for position
watched over by the masterful Bath House
from its prominent location overlooking the elegant central garden.

This tasteful mix of new and older buildings
from elegantly pretentious porticoes to plain and modest entrances
to homes
also demonstrates the former and the latest styles of balcony -
from timber filigree and wrought iron tracery
to concrete masonry with glass and chrome.

Whilst enjoying now the wide variety of simple modern pleasures
offered by this busy family-holiday seaside town -
the Crazy Golf, the pier's delights, the fresh-caught fish
and the palmist, Gypsy Lee's considered guidance for our time -
the observant visitor will also appreciate
the visible reminiscences and tangible souvenirs
offered by the backdrop of its architectural treasures
and imagine there the bustle of previous sea air takers
promenading in the sunshine of society
when Bognor earned its Regis in its prime.

Maureen Horne

WHEN I CAME UP TO BIRMINGHAM

When I came up to Birmingham one Sunday in September,
All the ladies wore brown coats, now, that's what I remember.
Headscarves covered up their hair as rain fell from the sky,
And all those ladies wore brown boots as they splashed by.

The road was up in Deritend, the mud splashed far and wide.
I whispered to my travelling friend, 'Oh let us go and hide -
Let's go back to London on the next fast train.'
But, I stayed here in Birmingham and ne'er went back again.

Now as I walk in Birmingham, I see the new green leaves
And brave new buildings reaching tall with pigeons in the eaves.
The ladies dress in latest mode, the girls are smart and fair,
The shops are full of fashions with beauty everywhere.

Yes, I made my home in Birmingham, that's the strangest part -
When you make friends in Birmingham, they take you to their hearts.
Visitors from far and wide are welcomed to the city -
That has its roots in industry and countryside so pretty.

One day if you have time, just walk and look my friend
As though you are a tourist, reaching journey's end,
Investigate the history and stories of your town
'Cause that's what I've been doing, since the rain came down.

Kay Liepins

THE BEST HOLIDAY

Eyes are lured by holiday brochures
Cities, coastlines, creatures and beaches
Decisions decrease as choices grow
Wander far or within stone's throw.

Visit again that seen before
Florida, Alps and Bangladore
Or traverse to horizons new
Geyser gush or winery view.

Need for a holiday increases
As a break from reading brochures
Decide to lounge with the radio
And enjoy tea on the patio.

Tired to fly, sail or motor
Time to avoid life's helter-skelter
Closing an eye, my world is carefree
Contemplating places I could be.

Years spent travelling continents
Memoirs of visual redolence
Yet today trades the best of any
At home, peace not costing a penny.

P A Findlay

Summer's Gone

Summer's drawn to a close
The air is cooling down
A lull before the winter
The leaves are turning brown

Wildlife ready to hide away
In a warm cosy place
Not until the weather warms
Will they then show their face

In the sky there are lots of 'V's
Seagulls flying south
When you talk or when you breathe
Steam comes from your mouth

Soon the clocks will go back
It'll be dark by half-past four
It's time for central heating
Draught-stoppers at the door

Prepare yourself for winter
It's certainly on its way
Stay inside and wrap up warm
And you will be OK.

Neil Warren

WALKING THRU' AUTUMN

I'm coming out of my shell
I'm coming out of this hell
I've climbed back up that ladder
From which ten years ago I fell
I haven't sold my soul
Though these wasted years have made me old.

The leaves are falling off the trees
It's autumn once again
I spent the summer all alone
No one called, no one phoned
But the strength I have within
Will free me of sin
I won't give up!
I won't give in!
I'm learning to love myself again
Outside my window
Falls the sweet September rain
And the cold north wind blows
The end of the summertime
I'll reap all that I sow
I'm walking thru' this autumn
So the story goes.

Andrew Richardson

AUTUMN COVER

I am reluctant now to leave my bed
To leave my house and follow paths I tread.
I am cosy here in the warmth and heat.
Comfy beneath the covers, I retreat.

The sun needs more time to break through the fog
To soak up the dewdrops and warm the log
To encourage me to put on my coat
And to go walking through the autumn cloak.

A mantle of colour - golden and bronze
The pathways strewn with leaves and curling fronds.
A flutter of foliage as the breeze shakes them free,
Leaving behind a cold, barely-clothed tree.

Mushrooms and fungi sprout from old dead stumps
Squirrels forage for nuts in leafy clumps.
Birds peck on berries in bushes nearby
And the hedgehog sniffs and gives a deep sigh.

I am reluctant now to leave my bed
To leave my lair and follow paths I tread.
I am cosy here in the warmth and heat.
Comfy beneath the covers, I retreat.

Moira A Whittley

Goodbye To Summer

Summer has been, and it is almost gone
With wind and rain, and some sunny days.
September is here - that mellow month
When the sun is losing its powerful rays.

The nights are slowly drawing in.
Gardens are passing their best.
Some flowers are already over.
Some are getting ready to rest.

Vegetables have been dug up and gathered.
Tomatoes are ripening and turning red.
Fruit has been picked, bottled and eaten.
Families have been well fed.

Soon the trees will shed their leaves
After they change to a golden hue.
They carpet the fields and cover the lanes,
Autumn is almost due.

The churches have their Harvest Thanksgiving,
With golden grain, and fruit of the field.
The doors are thrown open for everyone
To see that God's harvest can yield.

The children have all gone back to school
In uniforms of grey, blue and green.
Carrying lunchboxes and dragging their feet.
A picture that is quite often seen.

In the north west, the lights start to shine out,
Along a promenade of seven gold miles.
Sixty-six days they are a brash sight,
Encouraging visitors to stay for a while.

Let us think for a while now that autumn is here
Of people who have no homes or food.
Of babies who cry of hunger and thirst
Living in hovels, dirty and crude.

Thank God, for His gifts of the harvest.
    The Earth that He has given us to cherish.
His love, that is given so full and free.
    Without all this, this world would perish.

Joan Smith

Leaf Fall

Drifting gently to the ground,
The rustle of leaves an 'evocative' sound,
Forming a carpet beneath my feet
Bringing back memories, nostalgic and sweet,
Of swishing to school through a bonfire of colour
The scent and the sound compares with no other,
Seventy years have come and gone
The beauty in memory lingers on,
This yearly miracle of death in such glory,
A tapestry of nature repeating the story.

A J Langton

WINTER STORMS

I strike gold when the wind is high -
    clouds like tall trees.
The wildest writing of the sky
scribbles words that suggest the free
    tongues of ancient woods.
I like it best when like a tree
the clouds branch into china-blue
    like my wanderlust.
Or Moon like honesty, thrust through
dishevelled clouds at its first phase,
    swims gilded westwards
into the lakes that paint its glaze
of immortelles - I dream crestwards

through the wind chill. I like the rain
    that fills a street with
clattering darkness like a train,
where lightning wipes windows spotless
    with a crystal hand.
Bright winds, dark rain! Winter's atlas
of harrowed skies! How without these
    could we relish spring?
The racket of the bursting seas
promises the largesse of groves
    thatching blue with green
and thatching silence with the roves
of sound whose crests run shadows clean.

Chris White

WINTER NIGHTS

Long hours stretch like eternity, to nowhere.
Shadows cast their eyes, long and bare
across the horizon, obliterating and light,
then sweep down to meet the rough site
of the unconquered land, still and forlorn.
The sky, dark as ink, laden with clouds.
They hang deep down, like hammocks,
ready to shed their load, ready to explode.
The scent of woodsmoke in every abode
like the ghost of its fragrance, it mocks
the silence of the long, cold winter nights.

Anna Elliott

WINTER

W hen autumn leaves have floated down
I t's time for winter to come to town
N ature keeps changing every view,
T he Christmas berries are shining through
E arly snowdrops follow then,
R allying to welcome spring.

Joan Hammond

Autumn Happens Gradually

The sap of spring has thinned the whole summer long,
The birds start later with their early morning song.

The leaves get brittle and suddenly without a sound,
The summer green foliage lies brown on the ground.

Autumn happens gradually with the shortening of the day,
Trees cut, nuts piled, fruit picked, bales of hay.

The morning chill, the thickening blood, the lengthening night,
Means that most animals will gradually drop out of sight.

I'm getting sleepy as I write this, soon it will be time,
For poets to close their eyes and hibernate sublime.

All winter long I will dream of what's to be
Then to wake up in spring and write a winter's poetry.

Alan Bruce Thompson

ODE TO THE SUMMER HAZE

When summer is approaching
With its promises of pleasure,
We admire nature's powers, and the beauty of our flowers,
And begin to think of gardening and leisure.

But what of that war with nature
Now part of every summer season,
That appalling human need to kill every b****y weed,
And bug and worm and aphid, beyond reason?

As the farmer and the gardener
And the councils, spraying and pouring,
Are out poisoning air and water, in our summer season slaughter,
All our allergy and asthma rates are soaring.

For many now, the summer
Means a mental haze from Roundup,
Or a painful nose, and sneezing, burning eyes and throat and wheezing,
And aching head, with cold wet cloth now bound up!

Who gave some people the right to do this
To the *people* now collected
Round this indoctrinated slaughter, affecting all our food and water,
While the habitat of Warty Newt's protected?

Margaret J Reichlin

It's Snowing!

'It's snowing! It's snowing!'
    The little boy cried
Wide-eyed with excitement
    At the whiteness outside

A blanket that covers
    As far as the eye sees
So pure and new
    Even covering the trees

'Let's go for a sleigh ride!'
    He's eager and keen
Spoiling the newness
    Leaving tracks where he's been

Sliding down hills
    Making snowmen
Throwing snowballs
    At his older brother Ben

Toes tingling with cold
    He doesn't seem to care
All this fun for one small boy
    Surely, it isn't fair!

Time for bed now
    The day has been long
He'll awaken in the morning
    To find the snow has all gone.

Joanne Hale

WINTER IS HERE

Winter is here and nights are drawing in.
After four o'clock it is dark, dusk begins.
By the fire old Ma soothes those ageing bones,
Another chilly day shopping she's spent, now sipping
Her companion, Scotch, tired, she groans.

Winds scatter leaves which have fallen from trees
Brought on by the autumn, laying way for new seeds.
As we walk along in our warm winter wear,
Exhaling breath freezes, when greeting season's air.

Out on every place, Jack Frost resumes his work.
Where the touch of his hand, ice settles,
Landscapes he transforms.

When the snow begins descending, if it does at all,
Then youngsters will have fun, through their play hours at school.
Biting winds, freezing rain, thawing hands over coal fire flames.

Make no mistake, we are at the final of the year,
Winter is here.

Kevin Welch

WINTER'S DAY

Winter's morning, what a beautiful sight
Snow-covered landscape, a wondrous delight
Winter sun, low and bright in the sky
Golden reflections, pleasing the eye

Birds all sit huddled in the trees
Swaying gently in the icy breeze
A robin gives out his merry song
Ducks trying to swim in the frozen pond

The squirrel knows there's nuts to be found
But he can't dig for them in the hardened ground
A song thrush we see, it gives us a thrill
Trees loaded with berries, he eats his fill

Mother Nature is doing her best
Giving plant life a well-earned rest
Slumbering, waiting under the snow
To welcome spring with its glorious show.

Barbara M Beatson

THE FOURTH SEASON OF THE YEAR

The fourth season sends out thoughts to the thinker
For many colours and powerful scenes has winter
Before us is the backcloth of brilliant white shades
Made in contrast to vibrant autumn glow accolades
As the light lessens and days grow darker like a cloak
Out come bright scarves and warmly dressed are folk
With the wind chill and temperature beginning to tumble
Perhaps there will be snow and, underfoot, the crisp crumble
Poinsettias bloom and holly berries fill the branches bright
Twinkling lights in the trees, thus making a wonderful sight
A red-clothed old Father Christmas is seen around the town
With his princess in a shimmering silver dress and crown
The colourful faces of the carollers at your front door
Glowing wishes of happy greetings of the season do pour
Then bells chime out the joyous message of Christmastide
Looking from your window to the white world outside
Just think of the shades of winter as you cuddle up in bed
And look forward to the colours of the months ahead.

Octavia Hornby

SUMMER BREEZE

As the evening emerges and heaves a great yawn,
The nightlife awakes to work hard until dawn.
Dark shadows transpire, conifers that silhouette the sky.
A summer breeze hits the senses and stops one being wry.
Moments like this are second to none;
Moments like this without starlight or sun.
For a brief moment you stand there alone;
Yet you know deep within that you're not on your own.
All this evokes the beginning of time -
When the life on this planet was so very sublime.

Darryl Kristan Benson

THE SUMMER STORM

The wind unleashed its fury
As the storm closed in fast
Screaming in frenzy
Its gale force blast
Leaves fell like confetti
From trees battered and torn
Rain cascaded in torrents
From sunset till dawn
Mountainous waves
An awesome roar
As the sea rushed in
And pounded the shore
Like demons demented
Scudding clouds passed by
Distant sound of a lone bird
With its mournful cry
At last the winds were spent
Trees stood tall
No longer bent
The sea becalmed
With a silver glow
Ships once more sailing
To and fro
From bright blue skies
The sun shone
As suddenly as it came
The storm was gone.

Brenda M Hadley

My Wonderful Summer's Dream

When I think about tomorrow,
And think about my sorrows
Those beautiful days
Those beautiful days
That can never, no never
Recall.
It came with a dream
A bright summer's dream
A bright summer's dream
I can never recall
When I look back
And think, it reminds me
I could be here today
Gone tomorrow
Like the wind
Gone like a dream
Then there will be no more sorrows
And my tears washed away
Then, there will be no more tears
Just for me.

P B James

WHAT'S YOUR WINTER?

Cold
Dark
Dull
Wet
Gloomy
That's how I feel!

What's yours?

Bav

WINTER PLAY

The warmth has left the winter sun
And days are now much colder
As darkness falls and night draws in
Jack Frost becomes ever bolder

The winter season is now here
So wrap up cosy and snug
With snow floating gently down
Creating its own white rug

Morning is here and children play
In this new fall of snow
Making snowmen, snowball fights
From the cold, their faces glow

As they play, the hours pass by
And night takes over from day
The virgin white fall of snow
Has turned ugly, dirty and grey

Children tucked up safely in bed
Before sleep, they silently pray
For snow to fall again that night
So tomorrow they can go out and play.

Lynda Heaton

Song Of Autumn

Sing on sweet robin
draw my attention to what you will,
my deepest reveries are broken
by your day-long autumn song.

Ruffle your feathers
as you sit on the bough blood-breasted.
Peer around with your bead-bright eye
and herald life's fulfilment.

Berries flame red,
brown leaves fall brittle and wind-blown.
Late flowers droop sadly shower-sodden
yet still you blissfully whistle.

Of growth matured,
fields shorn, wild nights hurrying in.
Frost-chilled, mist-shrouded morns
and coal-fire skies.

Sing on little 'passion' bird
whilst all you survey lies down to rest.
You leave me listening, tranquil and quiet
in the evening of life.

Daphne H Vaughan

CONVENING

The autumn leaves
are convening again;
crisp and brown
large and small.

Thrashed around
tree-lined greens
by herding winds,
grating into a
chill winter cry.

The wind drops,
white stuff falls
gently creating
a layer of time.

Godfrey Dodds

A Walk In The Park

You said you weren't cold,
as some windswept leaves
scuttled by
to huddle in a corner.

We strolled alongside the lake
hand in hand,
I joked that it contained piranha fish.

A happy couple passed by
arm in arm,
her eyes seemed to twinkle
in the fresh breeze.

An antiwar poster
flapped on a tree -
as if struggling
to set itself free.

A black Labrador
ran after a stick -
its owner stopped,
to use an inhaler.

A smiling woman
in bright red knitwear,
modelled for a painter,
in autumn sun.

Olliver Charles

Inspiration

Walking through the leaves
Under my feet crackling
The smell of damp grass
A new morning begins.

The atmosphere still dusky
Only a few birds chirping
A chill grasps hold of me
From a gentle breeze blowing.

The quietness refreshing
In my old sleepy head
Now autumn's been and gone
The trees all brown and dead.

As I continue to walk
Thoughts flowing through my head
A world of inspiration
Words waiting to be read.

Laurie York

WILD AND WINDY

The unseen witness,
Terminates the serenity of the scene,
With a powerful force,
Whips into action autumn's finery,
Nature uncontrolled,
A tempestuous marauder of catastrophe,

An element, whose strength can be felt,
Audible to the ear,
As it bends and shapes its passage,
Where leaves dance to its tune,
Fluttering, bending,
Swaying in the fury,

An invisible invader,
Over which man has no control,
Sylphs, participate in a dance of energy,
Changing in format from a gentle breeze,
Then instantaneously whipping up with such ferocity,
It causes structural damage,

Tree branches snap, like twigs,
Hurling themselves to the ground,
A demolition expert,
Which randomly exits from the still air,
And unpredictably returns once more to a calm state,
Having swept vigorously all in its path,

Leaves in varying shades of ochre and crimson,
Torn from their host,
Now lie scattered upon the ground,
The winds of change awaken in us a respect of nature,
And we witness the cycle of life,
Which interweaves with our own.

Ann G Wallace

The Sting

One day while picking flowers in the garden,
A wasp buzzed round me quite persistently.
And though I ducked and dived, just to avoid it,
That black and yellow cretin followed me.

I did not want that pest to land upon me,
For wasp stings, I know, cause a lot of pain,
So I shooed it off and took a swing right at it,
And it started buzzing round me once again.

Now it seemed that he had sent for reinforcements,
With another wasp, arriving on the scene.
It seemed they formed a dual attack formation.
Those black and yellows; really getting mean.

I did not think these wasps would ever leave me.
Not for anything! Not even love or money:
So I rolled a paper up; and then I swiped them
And I sent them to the land of 'Wax and Honey'.

J E Davies

SEASONAL TWILIGHT

Walking along a country lane,
Once white fluffy clouds now give threat of rain.
Crispy, red browns of hedgerows and trees,
Chill of the early autumn breeze.
Birds no longer chirp and sing,
They now look south, take to wing.
Watching leaves as they drift down
Forming a carpet upon the ground.
To come are days of endless rain,
Turning the countryside to mud again.
Rivers and streams begin to rise,
They'll burst their banks, be twice their size.
As only memories of summer remain,
        Time for cosy glow fire with dancing flame.

Virginia Aggett

BROKEN SMILES

The soul has many puzzles,
To gain the autumn land
The world has its own space
The golden feeling brings on broken smiles
And swings a breath of golden air.

The land beckons the thought of the horizon
Of the hours so precious,
In the curling skylines lie
In distant woods,
The moist of the clouds gives content broken smiles.

Peaceful is the world making pleasant smiles
Energising sunlight bright with hope of pleasure,
The sun is the soul of happiness
Makes the love through broken smiles,
Broken smiles of the land be untouched of the heavenly paradise.

Heather Aspinall

BUTTERFLIES

Butterflies here
Butterflies there
Butterflies everywhere
Dancing and fluttering in the breeze
Going from flower to flower
Looking so spritely
In their lovely colours
Then on their way to warmth and heat
Gathering their own little treats
Flying past my windows
On to better things
Then stay for a rest
Do come back next spring.

Mary Spencer

THE FLOW OF LIFE

The flow of life on this planet first begins
With the first breath of a babe, or arrival of twins,
Their lungs expanding as each baby voice is heard,
More breath brings more volume, amazing, so absurd.
The flow of life is a continuous breath stream,
So simple yet wonderful as a rhythmic dream
Generating an energy flow our life force to use,
Life is an adventure, to explore where we choose.
The flow of life is dynamic, spiralling spiritually too,
Life force surges forward, with vibrations in all we do,
The mind is awakened to this creative energy flow
Of infinite possibilities, discovering oneself as we go.
The flow of life is all around us in the universe everywhere,
Radiating this natural life force as we breathe in the air,
Facing daily dangerous elements universally we all share,
Experiencing each activity of life we soon learn to be aware.
The flow of life, universal energy we can all receive.
It is unending and endless until this planet we leave,
Travelling forwards, onwards, no backward thoughts of strife,
We climb an evolutionary ladder progressing in each future life.

Stella Bush-Payne

It's Nice To Hear

Sounds of running streams,
Sounds of endless dreams,
Sounds of reckless cars,
And the children's little screams.

Sounds that mean so little,
Sounds that mean a lot,
Sounds that I do hear,
But sounds that you do not.

So don't take sounds for granted,
Listen to every tone,
I'm sure it's nice to listen to
Your mother on the phone.

So don't be one for mocking,
Think before you speak,
The world's a funny place
And it could be you next week . . .

Viktor Blain

ANOTHER REFLECTION

The window sees
eyes every morning
upon your
parting its covers.

Like the caged bird
who sees in its mirror
another caged bird
reflected.

Peter Asher

NEW DAY DAWNING

Look at the sun clipping the trees
Turning green leaves to gold in the light
A beautiful dove alights on the roof
Peace and tranquillity, a garden at dawn

Everyone's sleeping, the day's just begun
Thank you Our Lord for this wonderful morn
The birds in the air singing their songs
Elegant swans flying overhead

Where would we be without moments like this?
To sit and enjoy the wonders of the Earth
This chance to refresh mind and the heart
Now is the time to embrace the new day.

Dawn.

Carole A Cleverdon

THE SHORE-BOUND SPECTATOR

Views the ocean blue
Mariners true
Swept by tide
Far and watery wide
Birds stare
Fish beware
The spectator is splashed
By foam stashed
In the sea's locker
By the unruly docker
Whose breath in the wind
Catching sails and fish fins
A sea of life
That became his wife
While ships swept past
Salt spray mast
Shore-bound by feeling
The sea's pull reeling
Beauty in the eye of a storm
Cold takes over from warm
The spectator stood
And withstood
Wind and spray
To become a statue that says
'Time's sea will claim
All who seek fame.'

Tim Sharman

Grace

Through hours and hours I work through the showers,
potting, pricking and planting the flowers.

With my best-dressed attire, my wellies look dire,
I so wish for it to be drier and drier.

At the start of it all, I'm in such a haste,
to be the best and start the race . . .
then I find out I've got no space,
my seedlings grow, as does the smile on my face.

I have bantams in the garden
they run at a pace,
my garden is growing and nature within
has got such a grace.

The movement, the feel, the smell, the colour,
the calmness it all brings
with each other.

I love my garden.

Sally Cocking

EARLY VALLEY

Early Valley grazes ewe
on the rich elixir mountain dew.
God's creation now so rare,
elusive is the mountain hare.

Early Valley grazes ewe,
the rabbit paw and the horse's shoe.
But tread you careful who raises there
for the timber dog and his were-stare.

Early Valley grazes ewe
on the rich elixir mountain dew.
Rich in vein - dark with pain.
Still the oaks and the yokel jokes.
    Early Valley grazes ewe.

Alan Dyas

See The Sunlight

I like to see the sunlight
All around me every day
So I can go out walking for a while
As my kids come along and play.

I like to see the sunlight
Feel it upon my back every day
As I watch my kids swimming in the sea
Without going too far away.

I like to see the sunlight
As we all eat our tea
For in the garden we will read each other stories
How dear are the sun and my kids to me.

Keith L Powell

THE GARDEN OF PEACE

Come visit the churchyard
Named 'The Garden of Peace'.
The Good Lord's presence
Is felt within.
Speak His name
And torch the flame
Of the love burning
Deep in your heart.
Doesn't matter
If it's bitter cold
You'll feel a warmth awaits
And though you are
A little child
You're welcome here inside.
So you've begun life's journey
Yes you have
You innocent cherished babe.
God keep you safe
And secure in His love,
Forever in the garden
Of the Lord.

David Ashley Reddish

WINTER

Leafless trees, no flowers in bloom,
Pale sunshine in the afternoon.
Muffled sounds, the air is still,
No tulip, rose, no daffodil.
Nature's speaking, loud and clear -
Miserable winter's here.

Sleet and snow come tumbling down,
Shoppers shuffle around town.
Icy pavements in each street,
Cold, wet faces, freezing feet.
Little laughter, not much cheer -
Miserable winter's here.

Days are short, each night too long,
Winter's iron grip is strong.
To frozen lakes and garden ponds,
Spring calls out, no one responds.
Just accept, but not in fear -
Miserable winter's here.

Brian M Wood

BLUEBELL WOODS

This special place where I do come to rest
Reprieves my mind from things I do detest
And captures me in reverie of time untimed
Fills me full of calm, my anger does disarm
And cleans all unrest from my heart
Then makes a space for me to pay visit to myself
And rest within the armchair of my mind
And view what makes me who I am and why
Sometimes I do cry and others fly with joy
At what my heart has viewed
Life's fullness and the journey's yet untried
With vigour I am revived after this gentle rest
From standing in the woods watching bluebells
At their best.

Susan E Powell

CONKERS

This afternoon, walking so fast,
I spotted a conker, lost in the grass,
so rich in colour, all shiny and new,
then I spotted another, another, a few.
I crouched to retrieve them, lost in a pause,
thought back to my childhood, playing outdoors,
racing with friends in autumn's soft glow,
picking up conkers and leaves as we go,
filling our pockets, filling our hands,
dozens of conkers looking so grand,
seeing just who collected the most,
counting them quickly, starting to boast.
Now as a grown up, older and wise,
I once again see them through a child's eyes,
shiny new conkers lost in the grass,
making me smile as I think of the past.

J P Henderson-Long

Summer Love

Summertime is the only time
When I get the chance to make a rhyme
Sitting down on my bed at night
The TV on and in my sight
Writing down what I feel inside
Makes me want to confide
In the special person in my heart
Who comes out top in my love chart

Knowing I have sixteen weeks to decide
Whether to stay on, run and hide
Summertime here pours with rain
Drives me to think I am going insane
Nothing to do except plan my life
Slicing my sandwich with a bread knife
Trying to keep fit, I eat, write and sit
While thinking of playing in the sandpit

Scotland's summer is like it's winter
Watching people get a minter
Rain and wind, sleet and snow
Thinking ways to make some dough
Wanting to leave home to make my dream come true
Where the skies are mostly blue
Summer down south is warmer and bright
Where everything I want is in perfect sight.

Garry Traynor

WAKE UP, IT'S SPRING

At last spring was in the air,
You could see and smell it everywhere.
The season had come to have some fun,
And arouse all that shared.

The sheep were there first,
As they leapt up and dispersed.
Then there were the rabbits, o' so joyful,
About being with them, so playful.

But the biggest event of them all,
Were the trees standing there so tall.
With new life after death to begin,
On their branches was a breath of skin.
The birds were chirpy awaiting this call,
To start their nesting in the safety so tall.
And there were the other four-legged friends,
Who were all cuddled up so as not to see them at both ends.
O' yes, the springtime was certainly here,
To call out them all this time of year.

K Thompson

ABSENT WITHOUT LEAVE

Grey skies assemble once again
And the picture of winter remains
The prayers of apathy fill the air
And last year's memory complains
The rain performs its winter tricks
From its curse there is no reprieve
When we check the calendar page
The summer is absent without leave

Even the birds sing out of tune
As they rehearse their early morning croak
Flowers have lost their colourful touch
Living partially in their midwinter coat
Looking out the window into the mist
Again our eyes can't believe
We see again the morning clouds
The summer is absent without leave

People will ask the same old question
Where has the summer been?
Is it lost in mid-Atlantic
Playing games on the warm Gulf Stream?
Another day disappears without the sun
Another day we moan and grieve
When we call the seasonal register
The summer was absent without leave.

David Bridgewater

SOAR

Feel the tears in your eyes
The sadness in your heart
And let it be

Feel the icy wind press hard on your face
Turning your ears to cherry-red
And let it be

Look at the world with new eyes.
Accept the good with the bad.
Look hard at the edges and watch them go smooth,
The wheel of life in another incongruence;
Like harsh wind against a clear blue sea,
Red lava over fresh green grass,
Quick death upon a newborn lamb,
The excitement when you say 'I am!'

Put out your arms and reach up high.
Now you can spread your wings and fly.
Embrace the world.

Katie Boyd

Daffodils

Daffodils nodding in the breeze.
Various shades of sunshine, to please.
They gladden the heart
Ringing out their song.
Flirting and dancing
On stems tall and strong.
Orange trumpets looking so bold,
Shy, tender petals crowning with gold.
Leaves of green, dressed like a queen.
Some are white and a lovely yellow.
Spring is here in bright array
Watching the daffs gently sway.
How they adorn a friendly vase;
Lifting the soul that it may pray.
Daffodils are heaven-sent that grace the woods,
Ascend our thoughts.
Mother Earth has charmed the sill
Doting on her saucy Dil!

Margaret Malindine

NATURE'S BEAUTY

The force of fire mountains, the pressures of the deep,
All of nature's creatures look wonderful in their sleep.
The beauty of the sunset, the panorama of the moon,
Even the worst of weather will be changing soon.

Her power can be terrible, the devastation can be vast,
But each time anything dies, something new will grow at last.
From the purity of a morning to a tired sunset,
Stop and see the beauty lest you do forget.

We're only visitors to this place, for a while, it is true,
Mother Nature's handed her care to me and you.
Once the beauty's been tasted the course is very clear,
We must be ever watchful lest it disappear.

From the majesty and the power to the terror and the strife,
All the good and bad things are part of the cycle of life.
We are but caretakers of this wondrous place,
Do what you can to help, you'll be saving the human race.

Sean Sessions

PRIMROSE: FIRST ROSE OF SPRING

Cheerful, upturned faces, your richly scented rosettes, grace, in company, alone, graveyard gardens, shaded meadows and steep-sided hedgerowed lanes. Shy, modest beauty, first rose of spring, pleated petals, single-flowered stem, bright yellow star, mist-veiled sun. Wood, meadow, hedge, etched upon your tongue-like leaf. Snowdrop thaw, daffodil wane, the bluebells breath in the woods again; winter, summer, floral link, the foxglove prince bids you sleep.

K J Hooper

THE SQUIRRELS

The squirrel is a tiny creature, so swift and full of fun.
He scampers up and down the tree, he can really run.

I watch as he finds a nut and holds it between his paws.
Then he sits down with his feast, and fills those little jaws.

When he's content and had his fill, up that tree he goes.
By this time he is joined by his mate who keeps him on his toes.

The branches they bend and crackle, he is quick to the chase.
They go higher and higher up the tree, then back down to the base.

People start to gather, amused by what they see.
The squirrels enjoy the attention and continue their frolics with glee.

The pleasure from a nature walk is too good to be true.
So get your camera and walking shoes. You can experience it too.

Barbara Russell

The Sea

I stand beside the shore
I hear the sea roar
I see the waves crash
I feel the spray splash
I'm in awe of its power
I sit and watch for hours.

Ann Elizabeth Bruce

MAGIC OF SPRING

Spring is a magical time of year,
New spring flowers begin to appear.
Trees bursting forth with the palest green leaves,
Gently swaying in the warm spring breeze.
A profusion of colours erupts from the earth,
Woodland creatures are giving birth.
Sweet scented blossoms of pink and white,
Open their petals in the early morning light.
Wood anemones carpet the ground,
Primroses and violets can be found.
Newly born lambs frolicking in the sun,
Their short life has just begun.
Catkins hanging from bare branches,
Little birds performing their courtshіp dances.

Zoiyar Cole

WHEN?

When does the droplet
become a shower of rain?
When does the shower of rain
become a puddle?
When does the puddle
become a creek?
When does the creek
become a river?
When does the river
become a sea?
When does the sea
become an ocean?
When does the ocean
become a droplet?

When do I become?

Michael Wilson

UNTITLED

Hung above the ash in the September sky
A beautiful orb, suspended, I espy
In the darkened east, a jewel,
Below Orion lie.

Sirius outshines all,
He is our brightest star
And, though from source his rays have journeyed far,
Communes with us with power.

His sturdy darting shafts of liquid light and hue
Speak of the gems that he bestows on few
His colours are ruby red, emerald green and sapphire blue.

V Jenkins

Ponds

Midnight, floating water lilies closed for the night
The odd water rat surfing, endlessly out of sight
Fear of the water was never present here
And for completion, a rippling moon, the perfect sphere.

Barbara Rumsey

WINTER

Is grey strands
Arthritis
Friends' funeral.
Sleeping alone,
Shelves of memory.
Soft solitude
And experience
Enough to blanket
The cold world.

Malcolm Currie

NATURE CALLS US

Awake, o' thou with slumber filled
Arise, shine bright thy mettle;
Come venture on the wings of morn
That e'er for thee are so adorned,
with beauty.

Come forth, lest flagging spirits grasp
A hold on melancholy's web;
Where merciless spinners wait to seize
The frail and captive souls,
of dread.

Come thou who doth despondent lie
Enwrapped in false security;
'Tis I thou cravest - soon thou'll know
Come forth and I will show thee.

Blanche Helena Hall

HOLIDAYS

Do you like to go on holiday
In hotels by the sea?
Eating dinners cooked for you
And drinking lukewarm tea?

Perhaps you like a caravan
On a modern site,
With luck it has its own mod cons
To save a trip at night.

Or do you like a cottage in the country
Far from home.
With paths to roam and farms to find
To buy food local-grown?

But maybe you like jetting off
To some hot, foreign land,
Where you fend off the mosquitoes
And get your skin well tanned.

Do you like lugging suitcases to
Railway station or airport?
Or sitting hours in the car
When in traffic you've been caught?

I like to stay at home, I do!
I know my house is cosy,
I love the comfort, in and out
Where everything is rosy.

My food is good and healthy,
I cook it all myself
I'll watch the places on TV
And see people spend their wealth.

Elizabeth Stevens

SUMMER'S FADING

Tractors judder, noisy engines crop season's yield
Gentle ripples, surrounding lazy flowing brook
Autumn harvest creates flattened blanket fields
Nature's winking that awesome wintry look
Horses scatter, running through evening's dimming glaze
Darting, swooping, birds dive-bomb them all
Cows chew damp cud in the late summer's haze
Hills tower high, grand trees stand tall
Seagulls fly landwards, so rough is autumn sea
Sleepy meadows entertain lonely grazing sheep
Birds who have no boundaries fly forever free
Baby lambs, through purple heathers peep
Balmy breezes dance across chilled autumn's air
Nature, you sweetest darling, so beautiful and fair.

Ann Hathaway

WINTER MORNING

City,
Muffled in dense grey fog.
Trees, roofs and chimney pots
Appear and disappear
In swirls of cold, wet clouds.

Birds perch,
Huddled on bare branches;
Cats curl
By hissing gas heaters;
Dogs crouch
Inside fusty kennels.

The sun,
A glaring circle, glows,
Pierces this thickening cloud,
Frees low city bridges
And calm river waters.

People,
Walking across park lawns,
Now patterned with shadows,
Pass by painted benches
Still wet with misty drops.

Audrey J Roberts

The Wind

It's there . . .
I know it's there,
But can't see a thing
However hard I stare.

Its touch . . .
Can be such bliss,
Warm and gentle
Like a floating kiss.

But when aroused
Feels rough and wild,
Teasing and taunting
Like a wilful child.

Its moods . . .
Swing high, swing low,
Sometimes playful
Then angrily blow.

Its voice . . .
A soft zephyr breeze
Becomes ribald roar
As it whips thro' the trees.

P J Edwins

INFORMATION

We hope you have enjoyed reading this book - and that you will continue to enjoy it in the coming years.

If you like reading and writing poetry drop us a line, or give us a call, and we'll send you a free information pack.

Alternatively if you would like to order further copies of this book or any of our other titles, then please give us a call or log onto our website at www.forwardpress.co.uk

Anchor Books Information
Remus House
Coltsfoot Drive
Peterborough
PE2 9JX
(01733) 898102